W9-AMA-449

Reef
Life

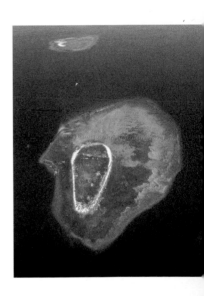

Andrea and Antonella Ferrari

Reef
Life

FIREFLY BOOKS

POQUOSON PUBLIC LIBRARY
500 CITY HALL AVENUE
POQUOSON, VIRGINIA 23662-1996

Published by Firefly Books
Ltd. 2002

© 1999 Arnoldo Mondadori
Editore S.p.A.
English translation © Arnoldo
Mondadori Editore S.p.A.
All rights reserved.
Printed at Artes Graficas
Toledo, S.A.
D.L.TO: 2010-2001

All rights reserved. No part
of this publication may be
reproduced, stored in a re-
trieval system or transmitted
in any form or by any means,
electronic, mechanical,
photocopying, recording or
otherwise, without the prior
written permission of the
Publisher.

First Printing 2002

Photographs:
p. 1: Pulau Mabul, Celebes
Sea, Malaysia
p. 2/3: Madoogali, Indian
Ocean, Maldives
p. 4/5: Al-Akhawein, Red
Sea, Egypt
p. 6/7: Layang Layang, South
China Sea, Malaysia
p. 278: Pulau Sipadan,
Celebes Sea, Malaysia

**Publisher Cataloging-in-
Publication Data (U.S.)**

Ferrari, Andrea.
    Reef life : a Firefly guide
/ Andrea and Antonella Ferrari. -- 1st ed.
[288] p. : col. photos. ; cm.

Includes bibliographical
references and index.
Summary: A comprehensive
guide to animals and plants
living in reefs around the
world including color photographs, dimensions, habitats, geographic area
and characteristics.
ISBN 1-55209-625-4 (pbk.)
1. Reefs. 2. Reef ecology.
3. Reef organisms. I. Ferrari ,
Antonella. II. Title.
577.789 21   CIP
QH541.5.C7.F47 2002

**National Library of Canada
Cataloguing in Publication
Data**

Ferrari, Andrea
    Reef life : a Firefly guide

Translated from the original
Italian 1999 ed., Tutto bar-
riere coralline, by Linda M.
Eklund.
Includes bibliographical ref-
erences and index.
ISBN 1-55209-625-4

    1. Coral reef biology.
I. Ferrari, Antonella
II. Eklund, Linda M.
III. Title.

QH95.8.F4713 2002
578.77'89 C2001-902622-6

Published in Canada
in 2002 by
Firefly Books Ltd.
3680 Victoria Park Avenue
Toronto, Ontario M2H 3K1

Published in the United
States in 2002 by
Firefly Books (U.S.) Inc.
P.O. Box 1338,
Ellicott Station
Buffalo, New York 14205

Printed in Spain

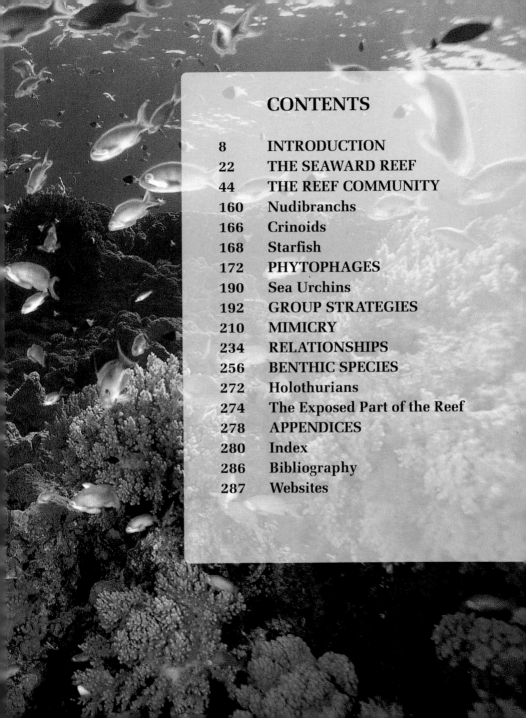

CONTENTS

Symbols

 Exclusively or primarily diurnal.

 Exclusively or primarily crepuscular or nocturnal.

 Can be observed both day and night; specific period of activity is noted in the catalog entry.

 Be careful. This species can be dangerous or lethal to humans if touched recklessly (ability to sting, poisonous spines) or aggressive under certain conditions (if disturbed or agitated). Generally, there is no danger when animals are left alone or, in the case of sharks, not approached during a feeding frenzy.

The entry for each species includes its common name, genus and species (e.g., Giant moray, *Gymnothorax javanicus*). Where it is considered of interest to lay readers, family names are also provided (e.g., the serranids, a family that includes groupers). Catalog entries are generally organized by environment and biotope. Within each chapter, individual species are then sorted primarily by family, except in the event of material differences in the distinguishing characteristics, behavior or preferred habitat of the species in question.

INTRODUCTION

THE CORAL REEF

The coral reef is an ecosystem without equal anywhere in the world. No other environment—not even the densest tropical rain forest—can convey so immediately such an impression of riches and vitality as is typical of an undisturbed and healthy reef. The transparency of tropical waters, their high luminosity at great depths, the inexhaustible bustle of innumerable creatures in every shape and color, the surprising and extremely delicate architecture of madreporic colonies never fail to astonish and fascinate even the most widely traveled observers.

Preceding page: Schooling Bannerfish, Maldives

The difficulties and costs involved in exploring the universe of the coral reef are amply repaid by its extraordinary, unique beauty.

The first traces of coral reefs date back more than 500 million years. Their distribution is remarkably varied over time, responsive in turn to phases of great geographic expansion and contraction following climatic changes that occurred during the different geologic eras. Today the distribution of reefs is limited to tropical seas, where reefs extend over a total area of nearly 600,000 square kilometers (232,000 square miles). Coral formations develop primarily between the surface and a depth of 30 m (100 ft) but only in waters whose average winter temperature stays above 20°C (68°F). Other factors that limit the development of coral reefs are water salinity, which must be constant, and the intensity of ambient light. Why are these three factors—temperature, salinity and sunny exposure—so important? If we think carefully about the reef environment, we quickly realize that the structural elements that underlie this ecosystem—those that help determine its appearance—are the so-called corals or, more correctly, madreporic colonies. These are admirably complex structures whose imperceptible growth and extraordinary fragility represent the very foundation of the reef habitat. At the simplest level, these coelenterate organisms can be described as countless tiny polyps (simple gelatinous "sacs" with an opening on

Gorgonians *Endowed with a skeleton that is elastic and horny, rather than rigid and calcareous, gorgonians (sea fans) usually tend to develop at medium and greater depths, far from the action of waves. As they are filtering animals, the colony always grows perpendicular to the current flow to optimize* *its exposed surface, which sometimes exceeds 2 m (6.5 ft) in diameter. It is not uncommon to find sea fans growing toward the sea floor or horizontally because the current, rather than light, determines the colony's orientation. The so-called sea whips of the* Juncella *genus also belong to the gorgonian* *group. The Alcyonacea (soft corals) and gorgonians both belong to the Octocorallia subclass, whose colonies' polyps all have eight pinnate tentacles each.*

top, ringed by tentacles) consolidated into a hard and fragile calcareous structure built by the organisms themselves: an exoskeleton (external skeleton) whose often bizarre but always functional shapes create the scenery of the reef. There are hermatypic corals that are able to build reefs slowly as the colonies expand and propagate themselves and ahermatypic corals, whose flexible framework does not lend itself to composite structures (like gorgonians, whose skeleton is composed primarily of a horny substance, and the so-called soft corals). Zooxanthellae are generally associated with the first kind; they are unicellular, symbiotic algae that live in the cells of coral polyps, averaging a million for every cubic centimeter of coral. Zooxanthellae furnish the polyps with caloric substances such as sugars and amino acids through photosynthesis (which explains the importance of ambient light). At the same time, they remove potentially harmful compounds like carbon dioxide, which could dissolve the colonies' limestone skeleton by converting to carbonic acid when it comes into contact with water. Coral polyps (easily pictured as tiny sea anemones) are not limited to using the zooxanthellae to procure nutrients. Indeed, they are endowed with extremely efficient weapons that allow them to paralyze and capture suspended microorganisms (plankton) that are carried on the current, especially at night.

The polyps' tentacles—just like those of medusas (jellyfish) and anemones—are thick with bulbous cells (called cnidoblasts) containing a thin hollow filament that is sharp and coiled like a spring (the nematocyst). The moment they contact prey, cnidoblasts open automatically

Coral Polyps *An individual* polyp *(in photos at left) embodies the living part of madreporic or stony coral colonies. Once distended, it looks like a pouch with a mouth on top, encircled by a crown of tentacles. Nematocysts found on the crown can often deliver a powerful sting, even to humans. The skeletal component at the base of the polyp into which the sac collapses during daylight hours is called the* calyx. *Its growth determines the colony's rate of growth. Branching corals can grow as much as 30 cm (12 in) a year, while spherical colonies confine themselves to a few millimeters (fractions of an inch) per year. Observed at night and up close, coral polyps not only offer images of exceptional beauty but also valuable details for recognizing the species to which the colony belongs.*

and jab their nematocysts lightning fast into the victim's tissue, injecting a toxic compound. The tentacles of the polyp then carry the dead or paralyzed victim toward the oral cavity and ingest it. Up close at night, it is easy to observe the tiny distended polyps that stud the surface of a coral colony by the thousands, projecting their tentacles into the current and waiting for likely prey.

Madreporic colonies assume profoundly different shapes depending upon the species that reside in them. In a typical coral reef it is fairly easy to find colonies that are laminate in structure (the classical tabular madrepores

13

of the *Acropora* genus), fingerlike (with short and stubby branching characteristics, as in the *Montipora* genus), branching (*Acropora* again), massive (the giant rounded "loaves" of the *Porites*, *Favites* and *Favia* genera, among others), brain-shaped or labyrinthine (*Diploria*, *Platygira*, *Turbinaria*) and even nonsessile (that is, detached from the substrate, as in the flat round colonies of the *Fungia* genus). In any case, every structure responds to precise conditions and often presents a serviceable refuge for a great number of different species such as fish, mollusks and crustaceans.

Not all coral reefs develop in the same fashion. Their shape and expanse vary according to wave action, the play of currents and their more or less rigid relationship with landforms. The basic structure is the so-called fringing reef, whose growth runs

Above, the image of a wholly intact reef in good health; the huge diversity of species contributing to its creation is evident (Layang Layang, Malaysia). In the smaller photos, two different kinds of coral reefs; above, a Caribbean platform reef (Los Roques, Venezuela) and, below, a series of atolls (Maldives, Indian Ocean).

Ascidians *These organisms—whose name is taken from the ancient Greek word for wineskins—are found as both colonies and individuals. They are filtering animals, like sponges and bivalves, that ingest water through an orifice on the upper siphon, filter it through a simple pharynx, and finally expel it through the lower siphon. It is thought that ascidians (sea squirts) may be the direct ancestors of vertebrates—despite their primitive character.*

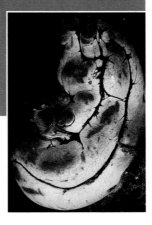

more or less parallel to the coast. In this form, the reef gives rise to an internal lagoon with a rubbly seabed separated from the open sea by a strip of coral whose summit lies at a very shallow depth and whose seaward wall (sometimes a soft drop-off interrupted by sandy terraces, sometimes a precipitous slope) hosts the highest number of species. Among the best known fringing reefs are the reefs characteristic of the Red Sea. So-called barrier reefs are an evolution of this structure and are typical of places where the continental shelf (or platform) moves away from land but continues to offer conditions that safeguard the development of madreporic colonies. The most famous examples of this type of reef—looking like a more or less oblong platform, composed of parallel structures—are found in Australia's Great Barrier Reef, in Papua New Guinea and in much of the Caribbean. Coral atolls embody the third model of reef development. Here, the progressive disappearance of a volcanic island leaves intact the fringing reef that surrounded it in remote times, generating an internal lagoon encircled by a more or less regular ring of coral. This structural type is generally found in open seas, and especially well-known examples are found in the Maldives Islands and Polynesian atolls. The extreme fragility of the reef's ecosystem is another important phenomenon that emerges from this short description.

Natural variations in water temperature, its transparency (the presence of sediments near estuaries), and its salinity (the huge intromission of fresh water near estuaries or following torrential rains) can limit or even interrupt its development. Irreparable damage is linked to human activities such as intensive fishing (shark, reef fish, seahorses and sea cucumbers for the food market and Chinese pharmacopeia, lobsters for the tourist industry), excessive coral removal (for industrial uses), the injection of polluting substances (related to mining operations, transport of toxic substances, cyanide fishing for the aquarium market, liquid sewage disposal from population centers), and fishing with explosives (practiced throughout southeast Asia). Unfortunately, all of this is happening in many of the places visited over the years by the authors of this book. Though many governments have officially assumed the protection and conservation of the reef environment, the damage is ever more evident and occasionally irreparable. Voices are being raised all over the world to protect this extraordinarily beautiful and important ecosystem before it's too late.

Facing page: One of the authors swims over a fragile tabular formation of Acropora. *Such extensive colonies—sometimes 2–3 m (6–10 ft) wide—indicate that the reef is still intact and in good health, but they are highly vulnerable to damage from typhoons and coastal storms.*

Coral Structures *Stony coral colonies assume a great variety of shapes whose surprising diversity contributes essentially to the reef's air of "articulated disorder." Over and above the species that belong to it, a colony's structure is strongly influenced by wave action and the intensity of currents to which it is subjected. More delicately branched forms and those with a leaf shape prefer to grow in deep and protected lagoons; this is true of the large globular colonies that sometimes form authentic micro-atolls several meters in diameter as the central nucleus dies off and the colony expands toward the edges. Colonies with short, robust branches that facilitate the feeding of polyps by slowing the passage of water have the advantage in turbulent waters.*

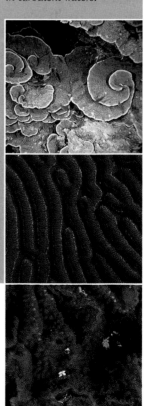

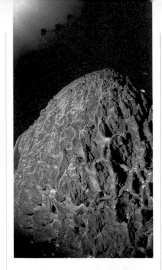

RED SEA

For European scuba divers, Red Sea floors represent the most interesting and economical opportunity to explore the universe of coral reefs. The reefs of this real and true ocean in formation are extraordinarily rich in life forms. To this day, a dearth of pollution and the low density of population along the Arab and African coasts have aided preservation of this ecosystem, with desert essentially lining their entire expanse. The unrestrained growth of underwater tourism, however, along with oil-tanker traffic and extractive industries in the north, is beginning to leave traces of pollution. The tourist sector is particularly advanced in several places along the northern Red Sea. Among the best known are Israel's Elat, Jordan's Aqaba, and Sharm El Sheikh and Hurghada in Egypt; all are easily reached and can offer visitors a high level of service. Tourism in the south is late to affirm itself and still reserved to an elite. Among the most celebrated

Sponges *With more than 10,000 species, almost all of them marine, sponges represent one of the most important groups of invertebrates. They compete with corals in more illuminated sections of the reef and occupy ecological niches at greater depths. They are filtering animals that suck the surrounding water into their bodies through countless tiny holes (invisible to the naked eye) and then expel it through a smaller number of bigger holes (called* oscula*) that are easy to discern (photos at left). Reef sponges vary enormously in size and shape and many prove surprisingly rigid to the touch.*

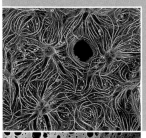

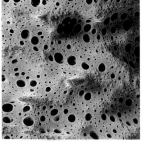

locations on the northern Red Sea are the Ras Muhammad promontory, now a national park; the reefs on the Strait of Tiran, rich in wreckage and historical remains; and those facing Hurghada. Near the border between Egypt and Sudan there are scuba-diving cruises and specially outfitted boats that permit independent excursions to authentic natural jewels like the pinnacles of Al-Akhawein and Zabargad Islands (in Egyptian waters) and the Sanganeb, Angarosh and Sha'ab Rumi seabeds (in Sudanese waters). Still other cruises motor through Eritrean waters

Soft Corals *Soft corals (Alcyonacea) belong with gorgonians to the subclass Octocorallia. The colony of polyps in these organisms is often of blazing beauty and is supported by a fleshy body whose texture is sometimes leathery (as in Sarcophyton and Sinularia)* *and other times flabby and semi-transparent. It is often "inflated" at will when a current is rich in nutrients (as in the genus Den-dronephthya). In the latter case, the central structure is reinforced by numerous cal-careous spicules (see detail at right). Soft corals defend* *themselves from predators by secreting toxic substances and hosting a multitude of guest organisms.*

and from Djibouti to visit the Dahlak Islands seabeds and the coastline of Oman, where native Red Sea fauna begin to trade places with those typical of the Indian Ocean. Richly engaging for experienced divers, the Red Sea can also be an ideal destination for beginners, thanks to the chromatic abundance of its seabeds and the presence of adequate facilities on land. Anyone looking for new sensations, however, should take a scuba cruise.

THE INDO-PACIFIC

The central Indo-Pacific basin (the area between Borneo, the Celebes and the Philippines) is by far the richest in species. To dive in these waters is to experience the ultimate in tropical marine biodiversity. Its scuba-diving destinations offer enormous variety, are expensive but perfectly organized, and often provide luxurious facilities. First from the west are the Seychelles' volcanic seabeds, followed by coral atolls in the Maldives, Indian Lakshadweeps—spectacular but often under assault by strong oceanic currents—and the Andaman Sea. Going east, the seabeds of Australia's Great Barrier Reef, a spectacular but sometimes expensive destination, are followed by those in Papua-New Guinea (visited almost exclusively on cruises), Micronesia (Belau, Truk, and Fiji—favorite destinations for Japanese divers), and Polynesia (Bora-Bora, Mooréa, Rangiroa).

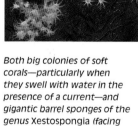

Both big colonies of soft corals—particularly when they swell with water in the presence of a current—and gigantic barrel sponges of the genus Xestospongia *(facing page, top) offer ideal subjects for underwater photographers, especially in crystalline waters.*

The Exposed Reef The exposed part of the coral reef includes stretches of reef that are periodically uncovered by the tides, the beaches themselves, the mud flats, and the mangrove forests closely connected to them. Such a variety of environments—and the nutrients they provide—cannot fail to entertain a wide variety of mammals, reptiles, birds and crustaceans. The mammals include wild boars and various monkeys such as the crab-eating macaque on land, and members of the sirenian family such as dugongs and manatees in water. Among reptiles intermittently associated with the reef, the monitor lizard, various semi-aquatic snakes and the dangerous marine crocodile, *Crocodylus porosus*, are worth remembering. Numerous tropical birds feed on fish. Among the best known are various species of pelicans (1), gannets and boobies (2), and herons (3). Among earth-crawling crustaceans are ghost crabs that inhabit tropical beaches and the gigantic coconut crab, *Birgus latro* (4), which has become rare throughout the Pacific.

One finally reaches the Hawaiian Islands and the rocky outcroppings of the eastern Pacific. The Indo-Pacific's western and eastern borders harbor a basin of tepid waters exceptionally full of life in the coral beds of peninsular Malaysia (Pulau Redang, Pulau Tioman, Pulau Langkawi), Borneo (Pulau Sipadan, Pulau Mabul, the Layang Layang atoll), the Celebes (the seabeds of Manado and the Bunakens), the Philippines (the ocean at Cebu), the Sunda Islands and, more generally, the entire Indonesian archipelago. Interesting photographically and scientifically, the area's seabeds are also distinguished by a variety of environments such as mangrove forests and silted estuaries that are more or less bound to the coralline ecosystem. The seabeds of the Indo-Pacific offer an infinity of interesting subjects, and some destinations are appropriate for beginners, thanks above all to the availability of reliable on-shore facilities. Its coral reefs are exceptionally rich in species and easily reached from land, usually without recourse to cruise boats. Nonetheless, the complexity of the ecosystem can only be fully appreciated by those willing to investigate carefully beforehand.

THE CARIBBEAN

Caribbean and tropical Atlantic seabeds (from Florida to Brazil, including archipelagos such as the Caymans and Bahamas, or single islands like Cuba, Bonaire or Aruba) generally host fewer species than the Indo-Pacific or Red Sea. People accustomed to the polychromes and variety of those waters will initially find the simple uniformity of Atlantic waters— a realm of pastel sponges and sea fans—disconcerting. Tourist facilities in the favorite American scuba destinations are generally designed for a choosy but frequently high-volume tourism, while cruises for divers aboard specially outfitted boats offer the best chance to visit remote seabeds like those off-shore Belize. The same can be said of the Pacific slope from Baja California to the gulf of Costa Rica. Land facilities are often designed for bulk tourism here, too, while the "live-aboard" formula provides

travel to isolated destinations (Isla del Coco, Revillagedo and Malpelo). The latter do require preparation, however, and a spirit of adaptation. What's more, significantly stiffer rules apply to Caribbean dives than to those at sites more on the "frontier." Caribbean seabeds are an ideal destination for beginning divers who do not want to forgo the comforts on shore and for more seasoned divers looking for less arduous dives.

The environment of the Indo-Pacific coral reef often plays host to various reptiles such as serpents, turtles and marine crocodiles.

Between Land and Sea *Belonging to the elapid family (the same as cobras and sea kraits), sea snakes are poisonous reptiles that are perfectly adapted to aquatic life. They wield a powerful neurotoxic secretion and have a distinguishing paddle-shaped tail. Some, like the* Laticauda colubrina *species (photo at right) return frequently to land, but others live a purely pelagic existence. They feed exclusively on fish and their eggs.*

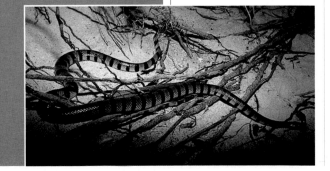

AN ECOSYSTEM IN DANGER

The reef ecosystem is found along the coastal strip of at least 109 countries in the world, yet it has been calculated that the coral reef in at least 93 of these has already been gravely damaged or even destroyed. Because of a series of diverse reasons, the coral reefs distributed over 60 percent of the Indian Ocean and Red Sea, 25 percent of the Pacific Ocean, and 15 percent of the Caribbean now risk disappearance. They would take with them an incalculable number of species including—in the last analysis—humans. We show in these pages some of the geographic regions where the reef is most threatened. At the same time we offer a few suggestions—which travelers must follow scrupulously—that are meant to protect the reef and minimize trauma to an ecosystem as complex as it is delicate.

Three images of fish markets in as many tropical countries. Intensive fisheries established by industrialized countries gravely threaten many species around the world. Other species, especially tropical ones, are subject to fisheries that still rely on methods that devastate the environment, such as the use of poisons and explosives.

OKINAWA, Japan
Huge quantities of coral are pulverized to make a "medicine" with supposedly miraculous therapeutic qualities. Naturally, the drug has no effect whatsoever, but extraction continues.

PAPUA NEW GUINEA
Black coral and the giant clams are prey for Japanese and Taiwanese fishermen, while the reef is seriously threatened by waste and hypersedimentation caused by the brutal deforestation taking place on shore. Turtles are overfished and fishing with explosives is common.

GREAT BARRIER REEF, Australia
Even though more than 2,000 kilometers (1,250 miles) along the coast have been declared a national park, the reef still suffers from the indiscriminate use of anchors, fishing and collecting of shells. Tourism has not always proved positive; in some areas, the visitors' habit of walking on corals has reduced the reef by 80 percent.

INDONESIA, MALAYSIA, PHILIPPINES
Intensive fisheries provide shopkeepers with live reef fish for aquariums and more recently for restaurants throughout southeast Asia. Massive doses of cyanide are scattered in the water to harvest less than 1 percent of the organisms present (the poison kills the other 99 percent). Turtles are actively hunted and butchered to furnish tourist restaurants. Everywhere, fishing with explosives devastates the reef.

THE CARIBBEAN
The reef is often threatened by urban waste, tourist infrastructure and uncontrolled fishing that supplies restaurants.

SRI LANKA

The construction of immense shrimp farms has brought about the ruin of coastal mangroves that are an essential habitat for many kinds of immature reef fauna. The destruction of mangrove thickets is a serious problem throughout southeast Asia.

ISLA DEL COCO, Costa Rica

Coral colonies are almost all dead following increased water temperatures related to the El Niño phenomenon. This is true for a long stretch of Central America's Pacific coast (which has no typical coral reefs, but still features sparse madreporic formations). Existing shoals of sharks were decimated to supply the manufacturers of a "drug" whose supposed anti-malignancy qualities have no scientific foundation.

GALAPAGOS ISLANDS, Ecuador

Uncontrolled fishing of holothurians (sea cucumbers) to supply Chinese merchants and restaurants around the world has caused the ecosystem serious damage. Arson fires have been set on several islands in retaliation against national park authorities.

How to Protect the Reef

DON'T purchase products made from turtle shells anywhere in the world. For the same reason, avoid buying souvenirs made from shark jaws, shells (especially tritons) or coral.

DON'T eat dishes prepared with the meat, eggs or fat of a turtle, including the famous soup. This is especially true for travelers in Indonesia and Bali where there is still a flourishing trade in turtle meat, targeted exclusively at tourists.

DON'T eat dishes prepared with shark meat such as the famous sharkfin soup. Every species of shark found in tropical and subtropical waters is in grave danger from fishermen who supply the world's restaurants.

DON'T eat lobsters in excessive quantities just because you can do so in the tropics. The appetite and provincialism of European and American tourists have brought about an alarming decline of this crustacean in almost all tropical waters.

DON'T buy traditional Chinese remedies, especially those prepared using reef animals. Beyond their doubtful efficacy (and occasional outright danger to one's health), the trade in them severely threatens many fish species, from sharks to seahorses.

DON'T walk on the reef, even in rubber-soled shoes. Every step would destroy the work of millions of creatures toiling over hundreds of years. Limit romantic moonlit walks to the beach, where it is also cozier.

DON'T touch corals and reef inhabitants when diving. Besides risking an ugly wound or allergic reaction, you could destroy a stony coral colony's hundred years' labor in a few seconds. For the same reason, be very careful where you flap your fins and how you move about.

DON'T carry off living or dead organisms from a submerged reef or beach. Things that seem marvelous in the moment will quickly start to smell and become decontextualized dead weight at home. Corals, shells and starfish are far more beautiful left where they are and, above all, left alive.

THE SEAWARD REEF

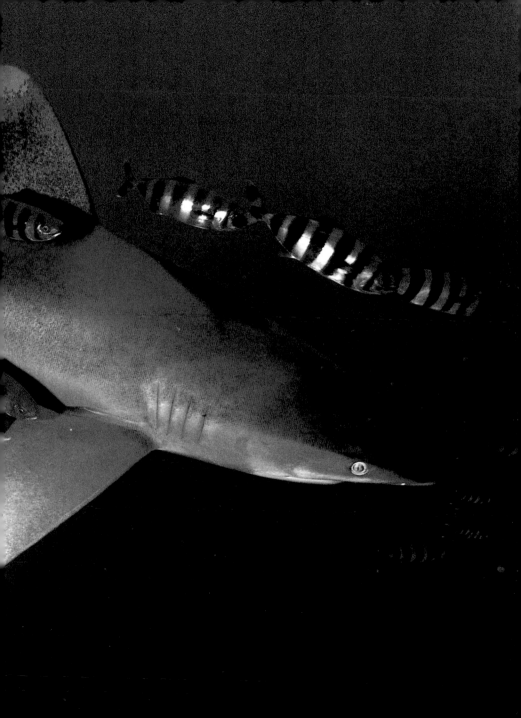

Preceding page: Oceanic Whitetip Shark, Red Sea

The strip of open ocean adjacent to the coral reef hosts a great variety of species that are generally larger than those that inhabit the reef Itself. Some, such as the Manta birostris *ray (at right), are pelagic in habit; others, such as the green turtle,* Chelonia mydas *(below), and to a greater degree the zebra shark,* Stegostoma fasciatum *(bottom), are more tied by habit to the coral environment.*

FROM THE OCEAN DEPTHS

Alternately a soft slope, a craggy drop-off interrupted by sandy terraces, or a vertical wall, the seaward or outer part of the reef is an irresistible attraction for many species of large marine predators. Some of them stake out a fixed territory and end up living their entire lives in the immediate vicinity of the reef. Others are largely pelagic; they spend most of their existence in the open sea and approach the perimeter of the reef only occasionally or to exploit special circumstances. Some end up bound to the ecosystem of the coral reef and never leave it. Among the pelagic group are marine mammals such as killer whales and dolphins, including bottle-nosed dolphins; reptiles such as turtles and sea snakes; large marine filter-feeders such as rays and whale sharks; and spotted eagle

An Essential Role *Overrun by the play of currents that carry great quantities of nutritive substances, the seaward walls of the reef are host to an extraordinary variety and quantity of living species—an abundance of prey that contrasts strongly with the "blue desert" of the open sea. By arriving from the ocean depths and climbing nocturnally from the deepest chasms, the large predators make swift attacks among the regular reef inhabitants—usually the older, slower or merely disabled individuals—to procure food for themselves while playing out their primary ecological role of weeding out the weaker members.*

rays and numerous sharks. These are spectacular animals whose appearance in the immediate vicinity of the reef will always kindle the interest of divers. Their arrival is generally linked to specific phenomena such as a large concentration of their usual prey or the mating season. Various bony predator fish (especially barracuda, carangids and tarpons) and some sharks (gray reef, silvertip) belong to the second group whose behavior is strongly territorial or more connected to the seabed (whitetip, nurse, zebra). Without exception, every denizen of the open sea is characterized by a powerful musculature (whose efficiency is optimized in certain tunas and sharks by endothermia or "cold blood"), a specially evolved hydrodynamic contour, and a sophisticated propulsive apparatus. Finally, they are almost always larger than true inhabitants of the reef.

The environment of the outer edge of the coral reef offers different species a great variety of biotopes. Often profoundly altered by currents and the undertow, the reef will be fissured by wide clefts and canals or interrupted by caves and fractures—the favorite refuge of predators such as the tarpon, Megalops atlanticus *(above). Alternately, it opens onto broad sandy plains, where big* Chelonia mydas *green turtles often like to linger (at left).*

A PERFECT MACHINE

Every form in the animal world corresponds to a function, and the large marine predators have developed survival mechanisms that are sometimes surprising. It is said, for example, that the characteristic cephalic lobes of various species of hammerhead sharks are tied to the sharks' ability to perceive even minimal variations in the electromagnetic field, a faculty employed in the continuous search for prey. As many hammerhead sharks feed on Rajiformes, the flattened contour of their nose may facilitate the search for prey hidden

on the bottom by operating like a kind of metal detector.

ESSENTIAL STYLING

In the vast immensity of the open ocean, there is no need for multicolored or flamboyant costumes. Instead, robust structures and an elevated hydrodynamic coefficient, propelled by a very efficient musculature and supported by reliable instruments of predation are useful to marine species. The shark may represent evolution's apex in this sense.

TO EACH HIS OWN

Every predator has a characteristic dentition to fit its prey of choice. Thus, the barracuda and high-seas sharks that feed on fast fish boast long, sharp teeth to catch and hold prey better, while those that favor larger species such as turtles— for example, the tiger shark—have large heart-shaped teeth that are serrated to better crush their shells. But there are also marine species of huge dimensions, such as many whales, the whale shark, or rays, that essentially have no teeth as we commonly understand them. They feed on plankton and small fish, filtering them directly from the water using the dense structures of baleen plates or gill arches. This type of feeding— enormous quantities of food secured with a minimal disbursement of energy—seems to be the most energy efficient and is the one most often adopted by massive creatures.

IN COLD BLOOD

Various marine predators, such as many tunas and several sharks, have evolved an extra mechanism to improve their hunting skills: their body temperature is a few degrees higher than the water in which they swim. This optimization of their bodily energy resources permits them to achieve higher speeds and faster reflexes when chasing prey.

Manta ray
Manta birostris

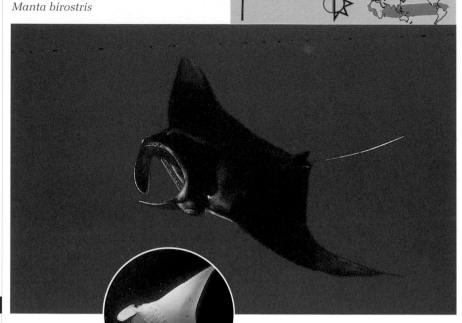

Range Circum-tropical

Habitat Coastal and pelagic waters, 1–40 m (3–130 ft)

Size Up to 9 m (30 ft) wide, typically 3–6 m (10–20 ft)

Description Biggest and most spectacular of the rays, completely harmless to humans despite its size and fearsome appearance (which won it the nickname "sea devil" in the past; its common name derives from the Spanish *manta* for cloak). Characterized by slow, majestic and elegant swimming.

Its ventral side is normally white, and its dorsal side is gray-blue or black. There are often darker spots on the underside or lighter ones on the back, their shape and position making it possible to identify individuals. Completely black or dark-colored individuals are not rare. By habit creatures of the open sea, they often approach the reef to feed on plankton massing on the surface of a current. This is a good occasion to observe the highly developed cephalic fins that are formed by an extension of the ray's enormous pectoral fins and through which it guides a "soup" of microorganisms toward its wide toothless mouth. Shaped like shovel blades, these lobes roll up along their own axes when swimming, improving the ray's hydrodynamic shape and assuming the unmistakable look of conical "horns" if the animal is swimming at a certain speed. When it finds itself in extreme shallows, the ray will often leap out of the water or strike the surface with the tips of its pectorals. Solitary by habit, it can sometimes be seen in groups of twenty or more. Generally indifferent but sometimes curious, it will often linger near divers and watch them closely if it is not bothered or frightened.

Devil rays
Mobula sp.

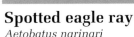

2

Range Circumtropical
Habitat Coastal and pelagic waters, 1–20 m (3–65 ft)
Size Up to 1 m (3 ft)
Description Various species of rays belong to the genus *Mobula*. More or less similar, they sometimes have a venomous barb at the base of the tail. Their outward appearance is nearly identical to that of a small manta ray (with a proportionally bigger head), and their habits are very similar though *Mobula* members prefer to swim in formation and it is rare to sight one alone.

Spotted eagle ray
Aetobatus narinari

3

Range Circumtropical
Habitat Coastal and pelagic waters, 1–40 m (3–130 ft) or beyond
Size Up to 3 m (10 ft) wide, generally 1–2 m (3–6.5 ft)
Description A ray of exceptional elegance easily identified by round white spots on its dark gray back and by its long, whiplike tail with one or more serrated, poisonous spines. Often seen in large groups over vast sand flats, it feeds on mollusks and crustaceans that it catches by combing the sea bottom. Very timid, it is a fast swimmer.

Oceanic whitetip shark
Carcharhinus longimanus

4

Range Circumtropical
Habitat Exclusively pelagic, 1–150 m (3–490 ft)
Size Up to 4 m (13 ft)
Description A big brown or olive-toned shark, immediately recognizable by its massive body and exceptionally wide pectoral fins tipped in white. Elegant in the water, deceptively slow, but curious and persistent; considered extremely dangerous to humans.

Gray reef shark
Carcharhinus amblyrhynchos

5

Range Tropical Indo-Pacific
Habitat Coastal waters, 10–280 m (33–920 ft)
Size Up to 2 m (6.5 ft) long
Description Territorial, usually gregarious, and in some places numerous along the reef wall. Normally very wary but often accustomed to scuba divers in the most popular locations where it can become aggressive. Its coloration is generally pearl gray on the back and white on the belly with a light stripe along its flank and a caudal fin lined in black.

Silvertip shark
Carcharhinus albimarginatus

Range Tropical Indo-Pacific
Habitat Generally pelagic, 10–800 m (33–2,600 ft)
Size Up to 3 m (10 ft)
Description Usually found near deep sandbanks far from the continental shelf; sedentary, normally wary, but often curious and potentially dangerous if stimulated. Diagnostic attributes include a robust body, gray-blue coloration and, above all, pure white edges on its fins.

Pelagic thresher
Alopias pelagicus

Range Circumtropical
Habitat Coastal and pelagic waters, 1–400 m (3–1,300 ft)
Size Up to 4 m (13 ft)
Description A fast, wary shark whose body temperature is higher than the water around it, observable only occasionally near steep slopes or the seaward reef of oceanic atolls. Unmistakable because of its scythelike upper caudal fin, which is as long as its entire body and is used by the shark to disperse and stun the schools of open-sea fish that it feeds on.

Reef whitetip shark
Triaenondon obesus

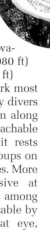

Range Indo-Pacific, tropical eastern Pacific

Habitat Coastal waters, 5–300 m (16–980 ft)

Size Up to 2 m (6.5 ft)

Description The shark most frequently sighted by divers underwater, common along the reef. Often approachable in daytime while it rests alone or in small groups on the seabed or in caves. More active and aggressive at night when it hunts among the corals. Recognizable by its characteristic cat eye, stubby snout, and white tip on its dorsal and caudal fins. Considered harmless but potentially dangerous if provoked.

32

Scalloped hammerhead shark
Sphyrna lewini

Range Circumtropical
Habitat Pelagic habits, 1–275 m (3–900 ft)
Size Up to 4 m (13 ft)
Description The most commonly observed hammer-

head shark in tropical waters, usually along the deepest slopes, often in shoals numbering in the hundreds. It has an unmis-takable and rather disturbing look. It is extremely wary, and approachable only with difficulty. This shark is very sensitive to sounds transmitted underwater and is easily irritated by divers' exhaust air bubbles. Congregating in enormous shoals is thought to be linked to mating rituals. The scalloped hammerhead shark's predilection for undersea peaks is attributed to their use of them as "radio beacons" during their long migration along the earth's invisible magnetic axes.

Tawny nurse shark
Nebrius ferrugineus

10 △ ◐☀

Range Tropical Indo-Pacific
Habitat Coastal waters, 1–70 m (3–230 ft)
Size Up to 3.5 m (11.5 ft)
Description Inactive during the day and often approachable while it sleeps in reef caves; actively hunts cephalopods and crustaceans at night. Its coloration is uniform, brown or hazelnut; its eyes are very small, and it has two nasal barbels. Potentially dangerous if bothered; its bite is tenacious despite relatively small teeth.

Whale shark
Rhincodon typus

11 ☀

Range Circumtropical and in subtropical seas
Habitat Coastal and pelagic waters, 1–130 m (3–425 ft) and beyond
Size More than 12 m (40 ft)
Description The world's biggest fish is harmless despite its great bulk. It feeds on plankton and small fish. A migratory species, it is observed punctually in various tropical coastal areas during spring months. Identifiable by its size, the distinctive white spots on its back and the wide mouth at the tip of its squared-off snout.

Zebra shark
Stegostoma fasciatum

Range Tropical Indo-Pacific

Habitat Coastal waters, 1–70 m (3–230 ft)

Size Up to 3.5 m (11.5 ft)

Description A nocturnal shark with an elegant coloration that varies locally in the intensity of its spotted pattern. Sometimes observable up close while it is resting on the seabed during the day. Like its close relative the nurse shark, it is considered harmless but still should not be molested. Immature specimens are adorned with vertical bands (which explains its common name).

Tarpon
Megalops atlanticus

Range Caribbean, tropical Atlantic Ocean
Habitat Coastal waters, gorges, caves, 1–12 m (3–40 ft)
Size Up to 2.4 m (8 ft)
Description Instantly recognizable by its characteristic silvery mirrorlike scales, its chrome-plated appearance and the oblique upward cut of its mouth. Sedentary; hunts at night and rests during the day with many others in the shelter of underwater canyons or caves. Can easily be approached if one moves with caution.

Great barracuda
Sphyraena barracuda

14

Range Circumtropical
Habitat Coastal waters, rarely pelagic, 10–100 m (33–330 ft)
Size Up to 2 m (6.5 ft)
Description This large, solitary and locally common predator is often curious about divers whom it will approach and follow. Despite its worrisome demeanor, the distinctive mouth with the projecting lower jaw, and its bladelike teeth, it is not considered dangerous and will flee rapidly if approached. It can vary its coloration at will by producing darker blotches.

Dogtooth tuna
Gymnosarda unicolor

Range Tropical Indo-Pacific
Habitat Coastal and pelagic waters, 3–100 m (10–330 ft)
Size Up to 2 m (6.5 ft)
Description Adults scour the edge of the reef in groups, attacking fish that have abandoned the safety of the reef wall. A predator of imposing size and audacity, capable of phenomenal accelerations. The authors have often watched it hunt and devour large specimens of *Caranx sexfasciatus* (see page 204).

Narrowbarred spanish mackerel
Scomberomorus commerson

Range Tropical Indo-Pacific
Habitat Pelagic habits, 10–100 m (33–330 ft)
Size More than 2 m (6.5 ft)
Description Another large predator of the open seas and trophy prey for deepsea fishermen. Usually solitary, fast and aggressive; observable along the seaward slopes of oceanic reefs. Almost impossible to distinguish underwater from its cousin the broadbarred king mackerel, *S. semifasciatus,* and from the wahoo, *Acanthocybium solandri*, both with very similar habits.

Bluefin trevally
Caranx melampygus

Range Tropical Indo-Pacific, Red Sea
Habitat Coastal waters
Size About 70 cm (27 in)
Description This fast and aggressive marauder habitually combs the outer reef making rapid strikes alone or in small groups. The iridescent blue color of its medial fins and bronze-colored speckles on its flanks differentiate it immediately from others in its genus.

38

Giant kingfish
Caranx ignobilis

Range Tropical Indo-Pacific
Habitat Coastal waters, 1–50 m (3–165 ft)
Size Up to 1.7 m (5.5 ft)
Description The biggest and heaviest carangid, its weight can exceed 60 kg (130 lbs). This fast, aggressive predator can be observed deep in atoll passes (the chasms that run between the lagoon and the surrounding ocean) or over sandy seabeds. Its dorsal side is olive-gray with silvery flanks.

Orangespotted trevally
Carangoides bajad

19

Range Tropical Indo-Pacific, Red Sea, Philippines, Okinawa
Habitat Coastal waters, 3–50 m (10–165 ft)
Size About 45 cm (18 in)
Description Identifiable by its gorgeous, completely golden coloration, more rarely tawny, yet always speckled in gold. Adults are generally observed alone or in small groups along the outer wall of the reef, from which they stray only rarely.

Bar trevally
Carangoides ferdau

20

Range Tropical Indo-Pacific, Red Sea
Habitat Coastal waters, 10–60 m (33–200 ft)
Size About 70 cm (27 in)
Description Prefers coastal reefs. Generally gregarious habits; younger specimens often swim near medusas (jellyfish) to exploit the protection offered by their stinging tentacles.

Yellow-spotted trevally
Carangoides fulvoguttatus

Range Tropical Indo-Pacific, Red Sea
Habitat Coastal waters, 2–100 m (7–330 ft)
Size Up to 90 cm (35 in)
Description Observable in small groups along the seaward walls of the reef or sometimes as single specimens mixed in with other species to better approach their prey. Like all members of the genus, it attacks its prey with sudden, high-velocity strikes that check their escape. Along with other carangids, it is frequently hunted by many sharks.

Pompano
Trachinotus sp.

Range Circumtropical
Habitat Coastal waters, 1–50 m (3–165 ft)
Size Up to 65 cm (25 in) long
Description Various *Trachinotus* species habitually frequent coastal reefs, lagoons, sheltered bays, and even push along in a few centimeters of water looking for the tiny mollusks on which they feed. Adults are usually gregarious. The pompano is silvery with blue-green shadings, but is chiefly recognized by its typically spheroid shape.

Pilotfish
Naucrates ductor

Range Circumtropical and subtropical waters
Habitat Exclusively pelagic, 1–30 m (3–100 ft)
Size Up to 60 cm (23 in)
Description Identifiable by its fusiform body and silvery color striped by five, six, or seven dark bands. It accompanies large species such as sharks and whales, feeding on the food scraps they cast off, and taking advantage of the "protection" these animals offer. They also use the pressure wave that precedes them to swim with less effort.

Bottle-nosed dolphin
Tursiops truncatus

Range Cosmopolitan
Habitat Coastal and pelagic waters, 1–40 m (3–130 ft)
Size From 3–4 m (10–13 ft)
Description This dolphin is easily recognized by its robust body and by a sizable separation between its forehead and its rather short beak. Its dorsal color is dusky gray. Generally found in small groups, it is extremely curious and intelligent but very shy and hard to approach underwater. Dolphins with longer, pointed beaks are also found in tropical seas.

Green turtle
Chelonia mydas

Range Circumtropical and in subtropical seas

Habitat Coastal and pelagic waters, 1–40 m (3–130 ft)

Size Up to 1.4 m (4.5 ft)

Description Superbly adapted to aquatic life, this reptile is an excellent and graceful swimmer that returns to land only to dig a nest and deposit eggs after mating at sea. There are normally around 100 eggs that hatch after about two months of incubation and the hatchlings immediately head for the water. In the course of that act, they register a series of geographic coordinates that will permit the few who survive to return as adults to reproduce in that exact spot. Identifiable at first sight by its wide, rounded head, its

blunt beak, and the presence of two prefrontal scutes between its eyes, the green turtle actually owes its common name to the color of its fat and not to its carapace, which is a brownish-olive color elegantly marbled with yellow. It feeds principally on marine phanerogams (*Posidonia*) and can easily be approached underwater. Though it is the object of many protective programs, it is gravely threatened with extinction because of habitat destruction, overfishing (especially in Indonesia), and the indiscriminate harvesting of its eggs as food.

Hawksbill turtle
Eretomochelys imbricata

Range Circumtropical and in subtropical seas
Habitat Pelagic waters and coastal reefs, 1–40 m (3–130 ft)
Size Up to 90 cm (35 in)
Description Easily distinguished from *Chelonia mydas* by its smaller size and the overlapping scutes that cover its carapace. The tip of its beak forms a sharp hook (thus its English name), and it can also be recognized by the beauty of its shell, which is marbleized with black, brown and yellow (heavily employed in crafting precious objects, especially in the past). Gravely threatened with extinction through persistent overfishing in various countries, it is primarily carnivorous and feeds exclusively on sponges and soft corals.

THE REEF COMMUNITY

THE REEF COMMUNITY

Visitors to the reef immediately find one of nature's most complex environments within its highly articulated physical structure. An infinite variety of microenvironments make up the coral reef, and every species has adapted with its own peculiar evolution. Since every form and color in nature—including the most eccentric and conspicuous—are ultimately dictated by laws of compliance with the environment, the richness and complexity of the reef have generated an awesome palette well known to every diver.

The complexity of the ecosystem typical of an undisturbed coral reef has generated evolutionary adaptations that are often sensational, such as the sweeping fins and flamboyant color patterns of lionfish in the genus Pterois.

Preceding page: Golden Butterflyfish, Red Sea

Butterflyfish (Chaetodontidae) feed almost exclusively on coral polyps and thus developed protruding mouth parts that function like tweezers. Their deep-bodied, laterally compressed shape allows them to thread through the dense branching of coral colonies with agility. Many species of butterflyfish are very territorial in habit, as are their close relatives, the angelfish (Pomacanthidae), so their appearance is most often intensely colorful and "semiotic." The long, narrow body of predators such as the

Look but Don't Touch
Since a body covered with scales can easily be scratched and damaged by coral that can cut like glass, many fish—such as the morays—have evolved a smooth, tough skin further protected by a thick layer of mucus. If touched, however, this protective layer can be dislodged, opening the way to latent infections. Marine creatures must never be disturbed or handled!

For every environmental niche, there is a corresponding structure. Lizardfish (left) have adopted a fusiform body appropriate to the voracious predator's bursts of speed; angelfish (below) are laterally compressed to better flaunt their coloration and swim among the corals; soldierfish (bottom) sport the big eyes typical of nocturnal animals.

moray eel enables them to maneuver through clefts in the coral in search of prey. To protect themselves from the nocturnal stalking of moray eels—who rely primarily on their highly developed sense of smell to hunt—the parrotfish, who rest at night imbedded among the corals, have in turn evolved an unusual strategy. They secrete a cocoon of transparent mucus that wholly envelops them and cuts off every olfactory trace. The striped pattern and wide fins of the so-called

Though it is reasonable to conclude that every color and shape is functional, some reef dwellers wear coats that look simply like a spectacular and bizarre evolutionary whim.

cobrafish can seem pointlessly sumptuous at first, but the stripes render this predator barely visible in the dappled light of coral seabeds. The large pectorals block every route of escape to the miniature fish that are their prey. Every microhabitat is populated by species that are perfectly adapted to it. There are tiny fish and crustaceans that spend their entire existence within a few square centimeters, hidden and protected by the tangle of the stony coral colonies' strong branches. Others pass their lives fluttering nervously from one perch

to another at the top of the reef, exposed to transient predators. Some other species—such as certain small rays or triggerfish—prefer the microenvironment offered by sand flats that interrupt the uniformity of the reef; they become more vulnerable to ambush but are better able to feed themselves. Like most fish that feed primarily on invertebrates (puffers and trunkfish

are also in this group), they have evolved an especially powerful set of teeth. These are just some of the numerous examples of niche adaptation. Careful observation of each species' behavior cannot help but yield others since we are far from having clarified all the complex ties and relationships that operate among inhabitants of the reef and their surroundings.

Many species typical of the coral reef, such as these butterflyfish (Chaetodontidae) (above), live as established pairs, and their union can sometimes last for many years.

Shape and Substance
Groupers (below) most often have a stubby, robust body. They often hunt by ambush and hover motionless in caves for long stretches. Cornetfish (lower right), have long, narrow bodies that are ideal for life in open waters. They are also predators, but have developed different strategies. It is not hard to identify a fish's habits by carefully observing its shape.

A COMPLEX UNIVERSE

The hundreds of different species that currently populate the coral reef occupy microenvironments that vary greatly from one another, and they have perfected highly differentiated evolutionary adaptations in response. The less-evolved reef fish are called malacopterygians or soft-finned (fish, such as the moray eels, whose fins are not supported by bony rays). Those considered more evolved are called acanthopterygian or spiny-finned; their fins feature bony rays that betoken a better adaptation to the environment.

Their appearance is recent, dating back about 140 million years.

RESEARCHERS
Many species that are peculiarly linked to the coral environment have achieved such high levels of specialization that they could not survive if moved to another.

Among the first researchers to dedicate themselves to the study and classification of reef fish were the French Bernard Germain Lacépède with his Histoire Naturelle des Poisson (1798–1803), and Georges Cuvier and Achille Valenciennes (22 volumes from 1828 to 1849), the Dutch Peter Bleeker with his Ichthyologic Atlas of the Dutch East Indies (1862–1877), the German Eduard Ruppell (1794–1884), and the Danish Petrus Forsskal (1775).

BIODIVERSITY
How many fish can normally live together in a defined expanse of coral reef? An Israeli scientific expedition captured 2,200 specimens belonging to 128 different species with a biomass of more than 136 kg (300 lbs) in a stretch of reef 150 m (490 ft) long, 3 m (10 ft) deep, and 22 m (72 ft) from shore. On other occasions, between 70 and 80 species have been classified in coral masses that were no more than 3 m (10 ft) in diameter.

INTERPRETATIONS
Despite the many field studies carried out in the world's tropical seas, several aspects of life on the reef are still far from being understood. Why does the coloration of some species seem to exist only to call attention to the animal? In some cases, the intensity of the colors appears to be tied to a function of sexual attraction, but in others, it seems inexplicable, at least for now.

Bluespotted ribbontail ray
Taeniura lymna

27 △ ✡

Range Tropical Indo-Pacific, Red Sea

Habitat Coastal waters, 2–30 m (7–100 ft)

Size Up to 30 cm (12 in) and to 70 cm (27 in) with tail

Description Unmistakable in its mustard-colored body studded with electric blue spots, this is the most prevalent ray on the reef. During the day, it rests among madreporic formations. It has one—or more often two—serrated barbs on the middle of its tail connected to a poisonous gland. Its sting is agonizing and recovery is difficult.

52

Bluespotted stingray
Dasyatis kuhlii

28 △ ✡

Range Tropical Indo-Pacific

Habitat Coastal waters, 1–60 m (3–200 ft)

Size Up to 40 cm (16 in)

Description Very common on sandy and silted sea bottom far from coral growths. During the day, it burrows into the substrate and rests with only its eyes exposed. This species has a poisonous barb located about halfway along its lengthy tail.

Giant reef ray
Taeniura melanospilos

Range Tropical Indo-Pacific, eastern Pacific

Habitat Coastal waters, 6–100 m (20–330 ft) and beyond

Size Up to 3 m (10 ft), including tail

Description This large, spectacular species is recognizable by its remarkably thick body. Its coloration is variably gray or black, mottled with darker tones, and it has one or more poisonous barbs near the base of its tail. The sting not only causes abysmal pain but can be perilous. It is often seen at the bottom of the slopes or sandy flats at the foot of the reef.

Southern stingray
Dasyatis americana

Range Atlantic Ocean from New Jersey to Brazil
Habitat Sandy bottoms, 1–25 m (3–80 ft)
Size Up to 1.5 m (5 ft) wide
Description Brownish or olive-colored back, sometimes verges on black; one or more poisonous spines about halfway along the tail. Usually observable when immobile, half-buried in the sand during daylight hours; easily approached if one moves with caution. Like the rest of its genus, it feeds on crustaceans and mollusks that it flushes out by rummaging in the substrate.

54

Cowtail stingray
Pastinachus sephen

31

Range Tropical Indo-Pacific, Red Sea
Habitat Coastal waters, 1–60 m (3–200 ft)
Size Up to 3 m (10 ft), including tail
Description A large ray with a uniformly brown coat and a very thick body further characterized by a wide flap of skin on its tail, which makes it look like a flag. Rather active, it frequents the bottom of bays and estuaries, partially covering itself with sand while it rests on the seabed. It feeds on crustaceans and mollusks.

Giant moray
Gymnothorax javanicus

32 △ ✡

Range Red Sea, tropical Indo-Pacific
Habitat Coral drop-offs, reefs and slopes, 10–50 m (33–165 ft) and beyond
Size Up to 2.5 m (8 ft)
Description One of the biggest moray eels. During the day it is easy to observe, poking its head out of its burrow, flapping its mouth rhythmically to aid its breathing. Easily approached, it must not be irritated or provoked in any way as it can inflict severe bites.

Green moray
Gymnothorax funebris

33 △ ✡

Range Atlantic Ocean from Massachusetts to Brazil, Caribbean Sea, Gulf of Mexico
Habitat Various environments, mixed seabeds, 3–30 m (10–100 ft)
Size Up to 2.5 m (8 ft)
Description Widespread on a variety of seabeds—rocky, reef, and corroding, this moray is a uniform green to brown. Approachable during the day as it pokes out of its lair, it is a night hunter, relying on its sense of smell. Can inflict perilous bites if bothered, but usually quiet.

Yellowmargin moray
Gymnothorax flavimarginatus

34

Range Tropical Indo-Pacific

Habitat Rocky areas, a variety of reefs, 3–100 m (10–330 ft) and beyond

Size Up to 1.2 m (4 ft)

Description Often confused by divers with *G. javanicus*, but it has yellowish skin color, yellow eyes and a head less distinct from the body. This species is often found in wrecks; potentially aggressive and able to inflict ugly wounds if disturbed or agitated.

Masked moray
Gymnothorax breedeni

35

Range Indian Ocean

Habitat Reefs full of clefts, 5–50 m (16–165 ft)

Size Up to 75 cm (30 in)

Description Immediately recognizable from the dark "mask" that spans its snout, this species makes up for its moderate size with open bellicosity. It is quick to bolt out of its den to wreak excruciating bites on those careless enough to rest on rocks or corals in its immediate vicinity. The most common moray eel in the Maldives Islands archipelago.

Yellowmouth moray
Gymnothorax nudivomer

Range Red Sea, tropical Indo-Pacific
Habitat Coral parapets, 4–160 m (13–525 ft)
Size Up to 1.8 m (6 ft)
Description A species that grows to huge proportions with skin finely stippled in white and easily identified by the vivid yellow color inside its mouth. Rather common in Red Sea shallows and considerably deeper waters elsewhere. Easily studied up close but should never be provoked.

57

Slender moray
Siderea thyrsoidea

Range Tropical Indo-Pacific
Habitat Seabeds with rubble, 1–35 m (3–115 ft)
Size Up to 65 cm (25 in)
Description Whitish in color like its congeneric *S. grisea*, this white-eyed moray is a species generally limited to detritus-covered, sandy, or silted seabeds, often in muddy waters. Sometimes burrows in pairs or with other species of smaller morays. The morays of the *Siderea* genus often settle into hideaways made of old jugs, oil drums or even tires.

Spotted moray
Gymnothorax moringa

38

Range Atlantic Ocean from North Carolina to Brazil, Caribbean Sea, eastern Atlantic
Habitat Seabeds with detritus and reefs, 1–12 m (3–40 ft)
Size Up to 1.2 m (4 ft)
Description A mid-size moray easily approached during the day, characterized by a rather variable coloration, but always on a whitish background densely spotted with darker flecks. It is by far the most common moray on the floor of the Caribbean.

Chestnut moray
Gymnothorax castaneus

39

Range Eastern Pacific Ocean, from the Gulf of California to Colombia
Habitat Reefs rich in clefts, 2–40 m (7–130 ft)
Size Up to 1.2 m (4 ft)
Description A large moray whose head is usually greenish-brown and its body occasionally studded with dense white specks. An irritable species, it is potentially aggressive, but is easily approached during the day when it pokes part of its body out of the burrow. Like others in its genus, it has strong, sharp teeth with back-slanting fangs.

Laced moray
Gymnothorax favagineus

40 △ ✡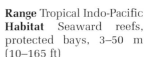

Range Tropical Indo-Pacific
Habitat Seaward reefs, protected bays, 3–50 m (10–165 ft)
Size Up to 2 m (7 ft)
Description This large species is recognizable by its flashy coloration with irregular black spots on a white background. Robust and peaceful, but capable of inflicting seriously painful bites. It feeds like all others in its genus on fish and cephalopods that it hunts at night using its faculty of smell and by deftly threading itself among the winding madreporic forms.

59

Fimbriated moray
Gymnothorax fimbriatus

41 △ ✡

Range Central Indo-Pacific
Habitat Reefs with sand and corals, 10–50 m (33–165 ft)
Size Up to 1 m (3 ft)
Description A less common species, observable on sandy flats with isolated coral formations. Often in association with cleaner shrimp of the genus *Periclemenes*. Identifiable underwater by its sharp snout and its yellow-greenish color that is lighter on the belly. Like other members of its genus, it has one or more rows of fangs down the center of its palate.

Barredfin moray
Gymnothorax zonipectus

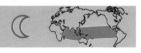

Range Tropical Indo-Pacific
Habitat Undisturbed sea-beds and coral drop-offs, 6–30 m (20–100 ft)
Size Up to 50 cm (20 in)
Description A small-size species, not very common, characterized by regular flecks and by the white marking between its eye and the corner of its mouth. It seems to prefer seabeds with abundant coral formations; appears exclusively nocturnal in habit and is rather difficult to spot during the day.

60

Ribbon moray
Rhinomuraena quaesita

Range Tropical Indo-Pacific
Habitat Seabeds with rubble, 1–55 m (3–180 ft)
Size Up to 1.5 m (5 ft)
Description Long, narrow body and bright electric-blue coloration accented in yellow at the tip of its snout. Immature individuals are black with yellow along the edge of the long dorsal fin; females are often completely yellow. Locally abundant but not especially common throughout its range.

Range Tropical Indo-Pacific
Habitat Coral and rubble seabed, intertidal zone, 0–15 m (0–50 ft)
Size Up to 70 cm (27 in)
Description Active in very shallow waters, sometimes observable during the day in tidal pools and even in rare cases when it slithers out of the water. Morays of the *Echidna* genus generally have duller teeth than the common moray; indeed, they feed primarily on crustaceans. Aquarium owners especially prize this species.

Chain moray
Echidna catenata

45

Range Atlantic Ocean from Florida to Brazil, Caribbean
Habitat Reefs and seabeds with rubble, 0–12 m (0–40 ft)
Size Up to 70 cm (27 in)
Description A species with characteristically blunt, conical teeth, it feeds primarily on crustaceans. Its coloration is generally brown or black with vivid yellow chainlike striations. Sometimes observable during the day while it hunts outside its lair, sometimes in tidal pools and very shallow waters.

Longfin snake eel
Pisonophis cancrivorus

46

Range Circumtropical
Habitat Shallow sandy, sedimented or rubbly beds
Size Average 50 cm–1 m (20 in–3 ft)
Description The Ophichthidae are eels with a smooth, muscular body and a rigid, pointed tail, which they use to scuttle rapidly into the substrate by swimming backward. Hard to individuate and still more to classify; its head sticking out of the sea bottom is the only part visible during the day. They feed on small fish and cephalopods.

Spotted snake eel
Myrichthys maculosus

47

Range Tropical Indo-Pacific
Habitat Rubbly and sandy seabeds, 1–30 m (3–100 ft)
Size Up to 1 m (3 ft)
Description A species generally observable only during night hours, when it roams the sea floor in search of the little fish and crustaceans it eats. Easily recognized by its white skin decorated by numerous round black spots, it is often mistaken for the sea snake, *Laticauda colubrina,* which is banded rather than spotted.

Spotted garden eel
Heteroconger hassi

Range Tropical Indo-Pacific
Habitat Sandy or muddy sea floors, 6–45 m (20–150 ft)
Size Up to 45 cm (18 in)
Description Members of the conger family gather in conspicuous colonies, their bodies rising from the sea floor like so many little blades of grass (from which they take their name "garden eels"). They feed on zooplankton carried on the current and withdraw immediately into the substrate if approached too closely. A similar and very common species on Indonesian and Philippine seabeds is the *Heteroconger perissodon*.

Variegated lizardfish
Synodus variegatus

49

Range Red Sea, tropical Indo-Pacific
Habitat Coral beds, 3–50 m (10–165 ft)
Size Up to 25 cm (10 in)
Description A relatively common predator, often seen lying motionless in ambush on the seabed, sometimes submerged in the sand or more rarely perched on an exposed roost such as a colony of madreporic *Porites*. Solitary or in pairs with a variable coat marbled in dark colors. Darts away if disturbed, only to perch at a short distance.

64

Blackblotch lizardfish
Synodus jaculum

50

Range Tropical Indo-Pacific
Habitat Sand or rubble sea floors, 3–50 m (10–165 ft) and beyond
Size Up to 20 cm (8 in)
Description The appearance and habits of this species are very similar to those of *S. variegatus*. However, it can be observed more easily on a seabed of sand or rubble at a certain distance from the reef and is identifiable by the prominent black blotch at the base of the tail. Solitary or in pairs, usually motionless on the sea bottom, but ready to dart away if disturbed.

Gracile lizardfish
Saurida gracilis

Range Red Sea, Tropical Indo-Pacific

Habitat Coral seabeds, 3–100 m (10–330 ft)

Size Up to 30 cm (12 in)

Description Although similar to true lizardfish in the *Synodus* genus, this member of the Harpadontinae family can be identified at first glance by its clearly visible multiple rows of teeth, which give it a truly unmistakable appearance. Very abundant, found in a large variety of environments; has a fairly variable background skin color. Like all other lizardfish, it feeds on small fish that it captures with a lightning-fast surprise attack.

Harlequin sweetlips
Plectorhinchus chaetodonoides

52

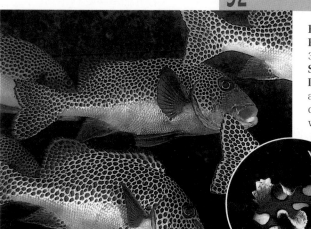

Range Tropical Indo-Pacific
Habitat Coastal waters, 3–50 m (10–165 ft)
Size Up to 60 cm (23 in)
Description Easily observed alone or in small groups during daylight hours when it settles in the shelter of big umbrellas of *Acropora* coral. Juveniles (inset photo) display behaviors and a mimetic coloration completely different from the adults.

Oriental sweetlips
Plectorhinchus orientalis

53

Range Tropical Indo-Pacific
Habitat Coastal waters, 3–50 m (10–165 ft)
Size Up to 50 cm (20 in)
Description Adults are markedly social and prefer the areas on the reef that are most exposed to the play of currents. The young are solitary and linger in the depths among labyrinthine coral formations. An easily approachable species favored by photographers for the elegance of its coloration.

Blackspotted rubberlip
Plectorhinchus gaterinus

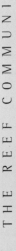

Range Red Sea, Indian Ocean
Habitat Coral drop-offs, seaward reef, 5–55 m (16–180 ft)
Size Up to 45 cm (18 in)
Description Like almost all of their cousins, this species feeds on crustaceans, mollusks and small benthic organisms, and prefers to gather in small groups during the day under the large umbrellas of the *Acropora* coral. Common and approached with relative ease.

Lined sweetlips
Plectorhinchus lineatus

Range Tropical Indo-Pacific
Habitat Coastal and seaward reefs, 3–50 m (10–165 ft)
Size Up to 60 cm (23 in)
Description Sometimes classified as *P. goldmanni*, it is easy to identify by its oblique dorsal stripes. Sometimes found in abundant shoals close to the slopes and walls of the seaward reef.

Lesson's sweetlips
Plectorhinchus lessonii

56

Range Tropical Indo-Pacific
Habitat Coastal waters,
1–50 m (3–165 ft)
Size Up to 40 cm (16 in)
Description Less common
than the preceding species,
it gathers in large groups
in lagoons or in caves
opening onto the reef's
seaward wall. As often
happens, juveniles are
more readily observed in
the shallows in seagrass
meadows.

Lemon sweetlips
Plectorhinchus flavomaculatus

57

Range Tropical Indo-Pacific
Habitat Coastal waters,
3–30 m (10–100 ft)
Size Up to 60 cm (23 in)
Description This species
appears to prefer coastal
waters near reefs and sheltered seabeds and is fre-
quently observed in turbid
waters and on sedimentary
beds. The young keep to
algal flats in lagoons and
estuaries where they enjoy
greater protection from
predators.

Giant sweetlips
Plectorhinchus obscurus

Range Tropical Indo-Pacific
Habitat Coastal waters, deep ledges, 20–60 m (65–200 ft)
Size Up to 1 m (3 ft)
Description The biggest of the sweetlips, often seen alone or in small groups at the foot of seaward reef slopes, on oceanic embankments or in the vicinity of shipwrecks situated at a certain depth.

Bluestriped grunt
Haemulon sciurus

Range Atlantic Ocean from South Carolina to Brazil
Habitat Slopes, coral drop-offs, 4–15 m (13–50 ft)
Size Up to 45 cm (18 in)
Description Rather timid, often gathers in small groups near the edges of reefs. Careful movement is needed to approach it. One of the most typical species on Caribbean seabeds.

French grunt
Haemulon flavolineatum

60

Range Atlantic Ocean from South Carolina to Brazil
Habitat Slopes, coral drop-offs, 2–12 m (7–40 ft)
Size Up to 30 cm (12 in)
Description Very shy, gregarious in groups composed at times of thousands of individuals along coral drop-offs. A retiring species demanding ample caution from those who wish to approach it. One of the most frequently observed species on Caribbean seabeds, and easily confused with *H. sciurus*.

Black-and-white snapper
Macolor macularis

61

Range Tropical Indo-Pacific
Habitat Coastal waters, 5–50 m (16–165 ft)
Size Up to 60 cm (23 in)
Description A species often observed near seaward reef slopes either singly or, more often, liberally concentrated and sometimes mixed in with other species like the *Naso hexacanthus*. Juveniles (inset photo) display long ventral fins and a coloration completely different from the adults.

Bigeye emperor
Monotaxis grandoculis

Range Tropical Indo-Pacific
Habitat Coastal waters, 1–60 m (3–200 ft)
Size Up to 60 cm (23 in)
Description Adults often gather in groups, sometimes in great numbers, during the day and in the shelter of caves near the seaward reef slope. During the night, the group disperses and single individuals visit deep sea floors in search of food. It is an easily approached species.

Twinspot snapper
Lutjanus bohar

Range Tropical Indo-Pacific, Red Sea
Habitat Coastal waters, 3–70 m (10–230 ft)
Size Up to 75 cm (29 in)
Description A sea bream of respectable size and formidable appearance, normally solitary but sometimes concentrated in huge shoals, especially during the reproductive period. Juveniles are more bound to coral flats, and to approach their prey, they imitate the behavior of Pomacentridae (or damselfish—small, territorial and harmless herbivores).

Onespot snapper
Lutjanus monostigma

64

Range Tropical Indo-Pacific, Red Sea
Habitat Coastal waters, 5–30 m (16–100 ft)
Size Up to 60 cm (23 in)
Description This snapper usually has one spot on the dorsal side, below the middle of the dorsal fin. Solitary or in small loose groups, almost always near a projecting ledge, a cave, or in the immediate vicinity of a wreck. The habits and appearance of juveniles are not presently known.

Dog snapper
Lutjanus jocu

65

Range Atlantic Ocean from Massachusetts to Brazil
Habitat Reefs of average depth, wrecks, 10–30 m (33–100 ft)
Size Up to 90 cm (35 in)
Description A timid, solitary species, hard to approach and observable in the most protected and shadowy parts of Caribbean reefs. Sometimes in the vicinity of wrecks, as well. The lighter triangular spot below its eye is diagnostic.

Schoolmaster
Lutjanus apodus

Range Atlantic Ocean from Massachusetts to Brazil, eastern Atlantic
Habitat Shallow reefs, 3–24 m (10–79 ft)
Size Up to 60 cm (23 in)
Description All of this snapper's fins are yellow. Frequently in numerous groups just a little above the reef, most often in the shelter of the big sea fans or colonies of *Acropora palmata*. Younger specimens find shelter in mangrove forests and small estuaries. This is another species characteristic of Caribbean waters.

Sailfin snapper
Symphorichthys spilurus

Range Western tropical Pacific Ocean
Habitat Coral seabeds, 5–60 m (16–200 ft)
Description Not particularly common; a large species characterized by its ornate coloration and by the nearly vertical cut of the adult forehead. Generally, close to isolated rocks and coral formations on large sandy flats; presumably territorial in behavior.

Bloch's bigeye
Priacanthus blochii

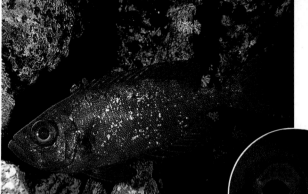

Range Tropical Indo-Pacific, Red Sea
Habitat Coastal waters, 3–30 m (10–100 ft)
Size Up to 30 cm (12 in)
Description Its skin varies from red (at night when this fish is in retreat) to silver (during the day) but this species can easily be identified by its big eyes and the oblique cut of its mouth. A similar species, *P. hamrur*, is differentiated by the lunate cut of its tail.

Sabre squirrelfish
Sargocentron spiniferum

Range Tropical Indo-Pacific, Red Sea
Habitat Coastal waters, 6–100 m (20–330 ft) and beyond
Size Up to 45 cm (18 in)
Description The biggest and perhaps the most spectacular of the Holocentridae, it has a robust pre-opercular spine (detail at left). Nocturnal, but easily observed alone or in company during the day, resting in the shelter of caves or ledges.

Bigscale soldierfish
Myripristis berndti

Range Tropical Indo-Pacific
Habitat Coastal waters, 6–50 m (20–165 ft)
Size Up to 30 cm (12 in)
Description Extremely common and adaptable, this species can be identified easily by the dark diagonal band just behind the gill plate and by the yellowish top half of its dorsal fin. Like other members of its genus, it is nocturnal; during the day, it rests in small groups inside caves and under ledges or in the shelter of cracks and crevices.

Shadowfin soldierfish
Myripristis adusta

Range Tropical Indo-Pacific
Habitat Coastal waters, 6–50 m (20–165 ft) and beyond
Description An unambiguous species characterized by its large scales and striking opalescent coloration. Nocturnal like other soldierfish, it can be observed alone or in pairs during the day, generally motionless and taking refuge in caves and tabular coral formations.

Tailspot squirrelfish
Sargocentron caudimaculatum

72

Range Tropical Indo-Pacific, Red Sea
Habitat Coastal waters, 6–50 m (20–165 ft)
Size Up to 25 cm (10 in)
Description Recognizable by its white tail during daylight hours, it assumes a completely red hue at night. Observable in numerous groups and easily approached in the most protected and least exposed parts of the reef.

Bloodspot squirrelfish
Neoniphon sammara

73

Range Tropical Indo-Pacific
Habitat Coastal waters, 2–50 m (7–165 ft)
Size Up to 24 cm (9 in)
Description Often in groups sheltering among branches of *Acropora* coral but also on seagrass meadows in atoll lagoons. It has nocturnal habits and feeds chiefly on small crustaceans.

Squirrelfish
Holocentrus ascensionis

74

Range Atlantic Ocean from North Carolina to Brazil
Habitat Protected zones along the reef, 1–15 m (3–50 ft)
Size Up to 30 cm (12 in)
Description Like all Holocentridae it is easily approached during the day, as it rests motionless in the shadow of ledges and refuges near the ocean floor. It feeds on benthic crustaceans and little fish.

77

Longspine squirrelfish
Holocentrus rufus

75

Range Atlantic Ocean from Florida to the Caribbean
Habitat Protected reefs, 1–30 m (3–100 ft)
Size Up to 28 cm (11 in)
Description It is rather easy to approach during the day while it hovers in the shadow of small caves or under *Acropora* coral formations. At night, it is more active, feeding mostly on small fish, crustaceans and mollusks.

Longjaw squirrelfish
Holocentrus marianus

Range Atlantic Ocean from Florida to the Caribbean

Habitat Deep reefs, 15–60 m (50–200 ft)

Size Up to 15 cm (6 in)

Description The most common squirrelfish species around deep reefs; like all its cousins, tied to the most protected areas of drop-offs and slopes. Observable by day in the shelter of small caves, fissures and cracks. Shy and difficult to approach.

Yellowstriped cardinalfish
Apogon cyanosoma

Range Tropical Indo-Pacific

Habitat Coastal waters, 1–35 m (3–115 ft)

Size Up to 9 cm (3.5 in)

Description Accessible in small groups in turbid waters within lagoons and estuaries, under large boulders, and on sedimentary and sandy seabeds. It is a sedentary species with clearly social habits, more active at twilight.

Ocre-Striped cardinalfish
Apogon compressus

78

Range Central Indo-Pacific
Habitat Coral seabeds, 1–15 m (3–50 ft)
Size Up to 8.5 cm (3.5 in)
Description A species with highly variable skin color closely bound to the microhabitat offered by the tight coral branching of *Porites cylindrica* and *Porites nigrescens*.

THE REEF COMMUNITY

79

Seale's cardinalfish
Apogon sealei

79

Range Central Indo-Pacific
Habitat Coastal waters, 1–25 m (3–80 ft)
Size Up to 10 cm (4 in)
Description Characteristic of coastal waters, often assembling in numerous groups among coral branches. Sometimes on sedimentary beds, even though it seems more common in clear waters.

Orangelined cardinalfish
Archamia fucata

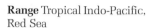

Range Tropical Indo-Pacific, Red Sea
Habitat Coral seabeds, 2–60 m (7–200 ft)
Size Up to 6 cm (2.5 in)
Description Often in dense groups at the entrance to caves or crevices, or among the branches of coral colonies such as *Porites cylindrica*, where members of the shoal find refuge when threatened. More active at sundown.

Large-toothed cardinalfish
Cheilodipterus macrodon

81

Range Tropical Indo-Pacific
Habitat Coastal waters, 3–30 m (10–100 ft)
Size Up to 22 cm (8.5 in)
Description Found on coastal reefs and in estuarine waters but also in the most sheltered points of the seaward reef, in clear waters, and on sandy bottoms. Bright yellow traces on the snout of adult specimens are diagnostic for identification of the species. Easily approached.

Blackstripe cardinalfish
Apogon nigrofasciatus

82

Range Tropical Indo-Pacific
Habitat Coastal waters,
3–50 m (10–165 ft)
Size Up to 10 cm (4 in)
Description Reasonably common in the most shaded areas of the seaward reef, coastal reefs, and in estuaries. Sedentary by habit, often in small groups. It is easy to get close to this species.

Five-lined cardinalfish
Cheilodipterus quinquelineatus

83

Range Tropical Indo-Pacific, Red Sea, subtropical seas
Habitat Coastal waters, 3–40 m (10–130 ft)
Size Up to 10 cm (4 in)
Description Quite easily observed in the typical habitats of other cardinalfish: protected and shady sites, small caves in the seaward reef, and along slopes leading to the open ocean. Often confused with the related and similar species *C. isostigma*.

Range Circum-tropical

Habitat Coastal waters, 1–35 m (3–115 ft)

Size Up to 60 cm (23 in)

Description An unmistakable predator despite wide differences in coloration—banded; horizontal stripes; yellow all over for the *chinensis* species found in the Indo-Pacific; and outright checkered in the Caribbean *maculatus*. Able to change color suddenly. Usually solitary, very common in coastal and seaward reefs, it often drifts head down in a vertical position to mimic gorgonian fans or "straddles" an individual of another species to approach a potential prey, unseen and shadowy. Trumpetfish feed by sucking in their prey, and because of their surprisingly roomy oral cavity, they can swallow prey that appear too large to pass through their mouths. Curious form and fascinating behavior.

Guilded pipefish
Corythoichthys schultzi

Range Indo-Pacific, Red Sea
Habitat Coastal waters, 1–30 m (3–100 ft)
Size Up to 15 cm (6 in)
Description Very common along the surface strata of the reef, in lagoon areas with detritus, and on madreporic colonies. Often in small groups or pairs.

Black-breasted pipefish
Corythoichthys nigripectus

Range Indo-Pacific, Red Sea
Habitat Coastal waters, 1–30 m (3–100 ft)
Size Up to 11 cm (4.25 in)
Description Closely related to the preceding species from which it can be distinguished by a generally brighter tone and even more by the darker area immediately behind its gill cover. Like all its cousins, it feeds on minuscule crustaceans.

Ringed pipefish
Doryhamphus dactyliophorus

 87

Range Western Pacific Ocean
Habitat Areas of detritus on sea floor, 1–50 m (3–165 ft)
Size Up to 20 cm (8 in)
Description Often in small groups, exclusively bound to the microhabitat offered by the spines of sea urchins in the *Diadema* genus, among which it finds easy refuge. Like all members of its genus and related trumpetfishes, it feeds on minute fish and crustaceans, which it aspirates with its pipettelike mouth.

Cornetfish
Fistularia sp.

88

Range Circumtropical
Habitat Coastal waters, 1–100 m (3–330 ft) and beyond
Size Up to 1.5 m (5 ft)
Description This predator rises to the surface at night and hugs the coast to hunt; easy to observe when attracted in large numbers to a light source. Its flattened body striped with intense blue is much more visible if seen from above instead of from the side.

Razorfish
Aeoliscus strigatus

Range Tropical Indo-Pacific
Habitat Coastal waters, 1–30 m (3–100 ft)
Size Up to 14 cm (5.5 in)
Description Almost always in small groups hiding near branches of coral colonies or among the long, thin spines of *Diadema* or staghorn corals. Immediately recognizable by their rigid bodies and characteristic head-down, vertical posture, which they maintain even while swimming. They feed exclusively on small crustaceans.

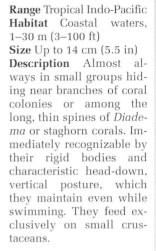

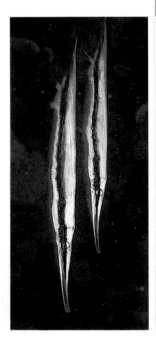

THE REEF COMMUNITY

85

Lionfish
Pterois volitans

Range Tropical Indo-Pacific
Habitat Coastal waters, 1–50 m (3–165 ft)
Size Up to 35 cm (14 in)
Description Also known as the turkeyfish or red fire-fish, this scorpaenid has a pale reddish body banded in white and wide dorsal and pectoral fins with long hollow spines attached to a venom gland. It can administer agonizing puncture wounds. Common in hollows and crevices and under formations of *Acropora* coral, where it rests in small groups during the day. More active at night, especially at sundown, when it uses its spread pectoral fins to corner small fish that are its usual prey, blocking every escape route, then sucking them into its mouth by creating a violent suction by suddenly opening its oral cavity. Easily approached, it is a favorite subject of photographers but if frightened, it quickly raises the festooned spines of its dorsal fins and flings itself at the invader. The scorpionfish's poison is thermolabile—it is diminished by heat, so the pain of its sting can be relieved by quickly immersing the wounded part in the hottest water possible.

Spotfin lionfish
Pterois antennata

Range Tropical Indo-Pacific
Habitat Coastal waters, 6–50 m (20–165 ft)
Size Up to 20 cm (8 in)
Description A very common species in the central Indo-Pacific; easily identified by the white-tipped, unconnected spines on its pectoral fins and by the peacock blue orbs that embellish the base of its pectorals. Its vertical bands are generally reddish or brown. Two tentacles festooned with alternating bands on its forehead resemble little antennas. It feeds on crustaceans and fish.

Radial firefish
Pterois radiata

Range Tropical Indo-Pacific
Habitat Coastal waters, 1–15 m (3–50 ft)
Size Up to 25 cm (10 in)
Description Easily recognized by its dark red or reddish-brown skin spanned by thin white vertical bands and by the long, white unconnected spines on the dorsal and pectoral fins. Apparently very sensitive to the sting-ing nematocysts in coral and therefore more common on rocky seabeds. Active at dusk, it feeds on crustaceans and small fish.

Ocellated lionfish
Dendrochirus biocellatus

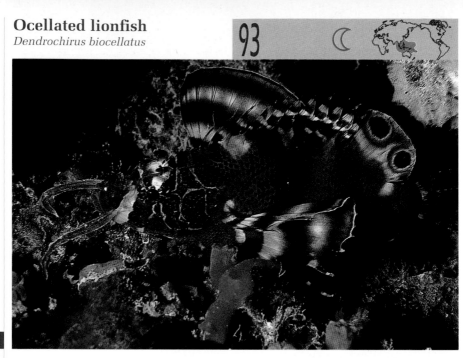

Range Indian Ocean, western Pacific
Habitat Coastal waters, 3–50 m (10–165 ft)
Size Up to 20 cm (8 in)
Description Nocturnal and nearly invisible during the day, very timid and usually solitary. Immediately recognizable by the bright coloration of its wide, fan-shaped pectoral fins, by the two ornate ocelli on its dorsal fin, and by the characteristic barbels on its snout. It is called the "Fu Manchu Scorpionfish" in some countries for supposedly looking like an elderly Chinese Mandarin. Rarely separated from the substrate on which it travels.

Zebra lionfish
Dendrochirus zebra

Range Tropical Indo-Pacific
Habitat Coastal waters, 1–80 m (3–260 ft)
Size Up to 20 cm (8 in)
Description Less anchored than its relatives to typically coralline seabeds, it is often found in lagoons with detritus or even sediment on the sea floor. Smaller than *Pterois volitans*, which it resembles at first glance, it is distinguished by wide, fan-shaped pectoral fins whose rays are joined by a continuous membrane. It feeds on fish and crustaceans.

89

Yellowspotted scorpionfish
Sebastapistes cyanostigma

Range Red Sea, tropical Indo-Pacific
Habitat Coral beds, 2–15 m (7–50 ft)
Size Up to 6.5 cm (2.5 in)
Description A minuscule scorpaenid linked exclusively to madreporic colonies where it takes refuge among the sturdy and typically rounded branches of the *Pocillopora* genus. It does not exit even if the block of coral is taken from the water. (For other species of scorpaenids, see the chapter on mimicry, page 210.)

Giant hawkfish
Cirrhitus rivulatus

96

Range Eastern Pacific Ocean from California to Colombia
Habitat Coastal waters, 5–23 m (16–75 ft)
Size Up to 50 cm (20 in)
Description Regularly sits motionless in ambush along reef walls, among the corals and in front of fissures or pockets. Easily recognized by its considerable size and hazelnut-colored skin crossed by irregular olive-brown bands that are outlined in an intense blue. Its pattern of colors blends well with the rocky seabeds in the eastern Pacific.

Arc-eye hawkfish
Paracirrhites arcatus

97

Range Tropical Indo-Pacific
Habitat Coastal waters, 1–10 m (3–33 ft)
Size Up to 14 cm (5.5 in)
Description Recognized by its red or hazelnut skin crossed by a lighter streak and by a multicolored arc behind its eye. Generally sits in ambush at the heads of coral formations of the *Pocillopora* genus, often with specimens of various ages in scattered groups nearby. If disturbed, it darts away and returns soon after to its usual perch.

Freckled hawkfish
Paracirrhites forsteri

Range Tropical Indo-Pacific, Red Sea
Habitat Coastal waters, 1–30 m (3–100 ft)
Size Up to 20 cm (8 in)

Description
A far larger species than the preceding one, easily observed while it poses in ambush at the heads of *Pocillopora* or *Acropora* formations and waits for the propitious moment to capture small prey. Usually has a dark purple or brownish dorsal color and yellow hindquarters. It is recognizable by its rounded head and fine speckling on its snout. If approached, it lingers motionless to the last instant and then darts away, only to return soon after to its usual perch.

Longnose hawkfish
Oxycirrhites typus

 99

Range Tropical Indo-Pacific, Red Sea
Habitat Deep coastal waters, 5–70 m (16–230 ft)
Size Up to 10 cm (4 in)
Description Generally observed in deep waters, usually perched on branches of black coral in the *Anthipathes* genus or on big sea fans. Seen at lesser depths only if its habitual perches are present. Sometimes in pairs on the same colony but always rather cautious and difficult to approach up close.

Pixy hawkfish
Cirrhitichthys oxycephalus

100

Range Tropical Indo-Pacific
Habitat Coastal waters, 3–40 m (10–130 ft)
Size Up to 10 cm (4 in)
Description A species that prefers shaded areas of detritus on seabeds or beneath reef walls, usually in shallow or medium depths. Territorial, active, wary, always hyper-attentive to its immediate surroundings. The intensity of its coloration varies according to water depth and the amount of light; completely red exemplars are not uncommon in deep waters.

Falco or dwarf hawkfish
Cirrhitichthys falco

Range Indo-Pacific
Habitat Coastal waters, coral drop-offs, 5–40 m (16–130 ft)
Size Up to 10 cm (4 in)
Description Territorial, generally in pairs on seabeds with detritus or among corals, often along the walls, and typically perched on its pectoral fins. Tufts at the tips of the spines on its dorsal fin are noticed right away, as is true for *C. oxycephalus*, the preceding species.

Fairy basslet, royal gramma
Gramma loreto

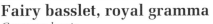

Range Caribbean, Bahamas
Habitat Seaward reefs, 1–60 m (3–200 ft)
Size Up to 6 cm (2.5 in)
Description A very timid species closely related to common groupers, with a splendid coloration. Often found inside small fissures, swimming upside down, orienting itself to the roof of the hollow where it is hiding. A common species in the Caribbean, it is a very popular aquarium fish.

Orchid dottyback
Pseudochromis fridmani

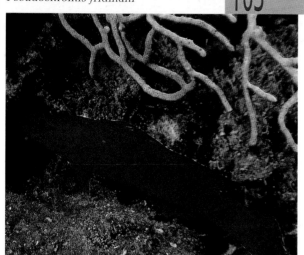

Range Endemic to the Red Sea
Habitat Fissure-rich coral seabeds, 1–30 m (3–100 ft)
Size Up to 7 cm (2.75 in)
Description Pseudochromids are generally small, territorial, diurnal, often characterized by splendid, bright coloration, and easily approachable. It is minuscule and incessantly flits around the immediate vicinity of its burrow, capturing the zooplankton on which it feeds with rapid darts in mid-water.

Diadem dottyback
Pseudochromis diadema

104

Range Malaysia, Philippines
Habitat Coastal waters, 5–25 m (16–80 ft)
Size Up to 6 cm (2.5 in)
Description A species of great beauty but very timid. Observable as it swims in spurts along the sea floor in places rich with cavities and shelters where it is always ready to hide. It feeds on zooplankton and tiny crustaceans, which it captures in the water column.

Squarespot anthias
Pseudanthias pleurotaenia

105

Distribution Indo-Pacific from Malaysia up to Japan
Habitat Coastal waters, seaward walls, 10–150 m (33–490 ft)
Size Up to 15 cm (6 in)
Description A species that prefers deep water, generally observable around 30 m (100 ft). Unlike all its congenerics, it rarely frequents the reef's seaward slopes in large shoals. It is more often observed in small, scattered groups or even as single individuals, swimming in open water without ever straying far from the reef walls.

Peach fairy basslet
Psuedanthias dispar

106

Range Malaysia, Indonesia, Philippines
Habitat Coastal waters, seaward reefs, 1–15 m (3–50 ft)
Size Up to 9 cm (3.5 in)
Description An exquisite species that prefers walls and slopes most exposed to the play of currents and surface waters; they are often present in abundant shoals around coral formations at the rim of steep slopes. Immense clusters of various *Anthias* species present one of the most beautiful shows in the coral universe.

Goldie, lyretail anthias
Pseudanthias squamipinnis

107

Range Red Sea, tropical Indo-Pacific
Habitat Coastal waters, outer reefs, 3–20 m (10–65 ft)
Size Up to 12 cm (4.75 in)
Description Possibly the most easily observed *Pseudanthias* species from the Red Sea to the Indo-Pacific, usually massed in huge clusters containing thousands of individuals whose bright orange color contrasts superbly with the intense blue of surface waters. Tropical anthiases form large harems of females guided by one male, identified by the long filament on his dorsal fin. When he disappears, a female who suddenly changes sex immediately replaces him. They belong to the serranid family and are thus unexpectedly and closely related to the biggest groupers. They feed on zooplankton captured in the water column opposite the coral wall and never stray from its protection.

Yellowstriped anthias
Pseudanthias tuka

108

Range Western Pacific from Indonesia to Australia
Habitat Coastal waters, outer reefs, 10–25 m (33–80 ft)
Size Up to 11 cm (4.25 in)
Description A species often found in great aggregations near steep slopes and the rim of embankments where there is a current. Easily identified by their intense violet color. An orange-tinted and more pointed snout distinguishes males from females.

Yellowback anthias
Pseudanthias evansi

109

Range Indian Ocean, Andaman Sea
Habitat Coastal waters, outer reefs, 5–40 m (16–130 ft)
Size Up to 10 cm (4)
Description Very common in the Maldives and western Indian Ocean, this species of tropical anthias feeds on tiny crustaceans, which it captures in the water column facing coral drop-offs.

Red-cheeked anthias
Pseudanthias huchti

Range Western Pacific from Indonesia to the Philippines
Habitat Coastal waters, outer reefs, 3–20 m (10–65 ft)
Size Up to 9 cm (3.5 in)
Description This species' greenish color is relatively lackluster compared to other *Pseudanthias*, but it is animated by the fiery red bar adorning the cheek of adult males. Rather common locally and often seen in dense masses among coral formations near the edge of seaward reef slopes.

Lyretail grouper
Variola louti

Range Red Sea, tropical Indo-Pacific
Habitat Coastal waters, outer reefs, 3–200 m (10–650 ft) and beyond
Size Up to 80 cm (30 in)
Description Perhaps the most beautiful tropical grouper, unmistakable in its purplish and violet uniform. Less inclined than other groupers to hover in caves and fissures, it can frequently be seen swimming among surface coral formations and along coral drop-offs. Territorial, it eats fish, crustaceans and cephalopods.

Coral hind
Cephalopholis miniata

112

Range Red Sea, tropical Indo-Pacific
Habitat Coastal waters, outer reefs, 3–50 m (10–165 ft) and beyond
Size Up to 40 cm (16 in)
Description Another well-known species prized by photographers, unmistakable in brilliant red-orange speckled with electric blue ocelli. Rather small, it is common on pristine reefs. Sometimes present in small masses, easily approached if one moves with caution or when it is being attended to by "cleaner" fish.

THE REEF COMMUNITY

99

Leopard hind
Cephalopholis leopardus

113

Range Tropical Indo-Pacific
Habitat Surface strata of the reef, walls, 3–40 m (10–130 ft)
Size Up to 25 cm (10 in)
Description One of the smallest species of tropical grouper, fairly common but often overlooked. Timid and sedentary, it can be observed while it waits motionless and hidden among coral branches, waiting for potential prey. Though not visible in this photograph the species can be identified by a small black saddle on the base of the tail stem.

Slender grouper
Anyperodon leucogrammicus

Range Red Sea, tropical Indo-Pacific
Habitat Highly articulated reefs and slopes, 5–50 m (16–165 ft)
Size Up to 40 cm (16 in)
Description A rather wary grouper, it is relatively common where greater protection is offered by branching madreporic formations. Thanks to a striated coat, juveniles approach their potential prey by passing themselves off as innocuous labrids of the *Halichoeres* genus.

Graysby
Epinephelus cruentatus

Range Atlantic Ocean from South Florida to Brazil
Habitat Protected reefs, coral seabeds, 3–20 m (10–65 ft)
Size Up to 30 cm (12 in)
Description Timid, often resting on the seabed, common where small crevices and ledges offer some protection. According to some sources, this species should be classified in the *Cephalopholis* genus. Like other groupers, it is an ambush predator that feeds principally on fish, crustaceans and especially cephalopods.

Peacock grouper
Cephalopholis argus

116

Range Red Sea, tropical Indo-Pacific
Habitat Coastal waters, outer reefs, walls, 1–45 m (3–150 ft)
Size Up to 45 cm (18 in)
Description A rather common species on seaward reefs and near slopes, easy to observe while it cautiously skirts along the outcroppings of the coral reef. Active during the day and generally more timid than its cousin *C. miniata*, it can rapidly change the chromatic intensity of its skin. It feeds primarily on cephalopods and fish.

Roving coralgrouper
Plectropomus pessuliferus marisburi

117

Range Red Sea and Gulf of Aden
Habitat Sandy reefs and mixed seabeds, 10–50 m (33–165 ft)
Size Up to 1 m (3 ft)
Description The species is found in the Indo-Pacific; this subspecies only in the Red Sea. A big serranid characterized by a splendid costume that is rather variable in color but always spotted with blue, a robust body and a concave tail. Sedentary, territorial, sometimes observed inside shipwrecks or in the shadow of *Acropora* formations.

Saddleback coralgrouper
Plectropomus laevis

Range Tropical Indo-Pacific
Habitat Coastal waters, outer reefs, walls, 10–50 m (33–490 ft)
Size Up to 1 m (3 ft)
Description A large, showy species with a remarkably variable coloration (in addition to the one illustrated, another common phase is white with black spots), but generally identifiable by its big, jutting teeth. Approachable while it rests in the shelter of giant *Acropora* umbrellas, it feeds on fish, crustaceans and cephalopods, and hunts mainly at sundown.

Tiger grouper
Mycteroperca tigris

Range Atlantic Ocean from the Bahamas to Brazil
Habitat Slopes and drop-offs, 3–20 m (10–65 ft)
Size Up to 1 m (3 ft)
Description A splendid serranid whose costume is fairly variable in color but always characterized by nine darker diagonal bands that give it an unmistakable look. Rather timid, this big Caribbean grouper can sometimes be approached while being attended to by cleaner wrasses and crustaceans or while resting motionless on the sea floor.

Humpback grouper
Chromileptes altivelis

Range Andaman Sea, Western Pacific
Habitat Coastal reefs, lagoons, walls, 1–40 m (3–130 ft)
Size Up to 65 cm (25 in)
Description Juveniles are white with black polka-dots. Adults are grayish, with smaller, more numerous spots. Observable in areas of detritus and in lagoons, the species is characterized by its sharp snout and wide, paddle-shaped pectoral fins, which are moved in an alternating rhythm.

THE REEF COMMUNITY

103

Greasy grouper
Epinephelus tauvina

Range Red Sea, tropical Indo-Pacific
Habitat Slopes, outer reefs, coral drop-offs, 1–50 m (3–165 ft)
Size Up to 75 cm (29 in)
Description A typical, average-size grouper with a plainly spotted coloration that serves to camouflage. Rather common and easily observed while it rests motionless on the bottom during daylight hours. If disturbed, it streaks away toward the closest hiding place.

Starry grouper
Epinephelus labriformis

 122

Range Eastern Pacific from California to Colombia
Habitat Rocky outcroppings and crevices, 5–70 m (16–230 ft)
Size Up to 1 m (3 ft)
Description Typical of rocky bottoms and outcroppings or boulder-strewn slopes, this species is easily recognized by the ten darker bands on its body and by the bright blue and orange spotting on either side of its head. Like all its bass cousins, it feeds primarily on crustaceans and cephalopods, which it mostly hunts at twilight.

Brown-marbled grouper
Epinephelus fuscoguttatus

 123

Range Red Sea, tropical Indo-Pacific
Habitat Lagoons, channels, coral drop-offs, 1–60 m (3–200 ft)
Size Up to 35 cm (14 in)
Description A rather timid species and not very common, generally observed in clear waters and coral-rich reefs. It feeds mostly on fish, crustaceans and cephalopods. Very difficult to distinguish at first glance from numerous other species of the genus *Epinephelus*, all of which look and behave more or less the same.

Greater soapfish
Rypticus saponaceus

124

Range Atlantic Ocean from Florida to Brazil
Habitat Coral substrates, 2–18 m (7–60 ft)
Size Up to 30 cm (12 in)
Description A curious member of the sea bass family that can often be observed while it lies prostrate and completely inactive, resting on the bottom and sometimes even leaning on one flank. Solitary and more active at night, it can secrete a soapy mucus from its skin that is toxic to other fish.

105

Sixstripe soapfish
Grammistes sexlineatus

125

Range Tropical Indo-Pacific
Habitat Coastal waters, diverse environments, 1–150 m (3–490 ft)
Size Up to 25 cm (10 in)
Description A serranid often seen in the detritus at drop-offs, on steep slopes, in lagoons, and generally in all biotopes that can offer abundant shelter. Generally observed in caves and crevices. Like all soapfish, it can secrete a defensive mucus from its skin that is distasteful to predators and mildly toxic to other fish. The number of stripes increases with age.

Leather bass
Dermatolepsis dermatolepsis

Range Eastern Pacific from the Gulf of California to Ecuador, the Caribbean
Habitat Protected rock cliffs and crevices, 3–200 m (10–660 ft)
Size Up to 90 cm (35 in)
Description An extremely timid and difficult-to-approach species characteristic of deep waters. Some sources also cite an Atlantic species, often classified as *Epinephelus inermis*, which in reality does not seem to differ from the *Dermatolepsis* in any aspect.

Indigo hamlet
Hypoplectrus indigo

Range Caribbean Sea from Florida to Belize
Habitat Protected bottoms and coral drop-offs, 1–40 m (3–130 ft)
Size Up to 13 cm (5 in)
Description A small serranid easy to identify by virtue of its bright white-and-blue banded body. The hamlets typical of Caribbean waters are represented by numerous species with varying color tones and markings, but some ichthyologists consider them members of a single species, *Hypoplectrus unicolor*.

Harlequin bass
Serranus tigrinus

Range Atlantic Ocean from Florida to Bermuda
Habitat Rocky areas and seagrass flats, 0.5–40 m (1.5–150 ft)
Size Up to 10 cm (4 in)
Description Very common on rocky bottoms and in seagrass meadows and rather curious. Easily approached as it forages along the bottom for small crustaceans.

107

Mexican hogfish
Bodianus diplotaenia

Range Eastern Pacific from the Gulf of California to Chile
Habitat Coral seabeds and rocky areas, 2–70 m (7–230 ft)
Size Up to 80 cm (31 in)
Description Wrasses are labrids whose *rufus* and *pulchellus* species are also found in Caribbean waters. A very active species near the bottom, recognizable by the labrids' characteristic swimming in spurts and glides (governed by pectoral fins). The young carry out a cleaning function in relation to other larger species.

Blue chromis
Chromis cyanea

Range Caribbean Sea, Bermuda
Habitat Reefs and coral drop-offs, 5–25 m (16–80 ft)
Size Up to 10 cm (4 in)
Description Very common in the water column above the reef and easily observed in large, loose aggregations while feeding on zooplankton.

Blue-green chromis
Chromis viridis

Range Red Sea, tropical Indo-Pacific
Habitat Shallow reef waters, 0.5–12 m (1.5–40 ft)
Size Up to 7 cm (2.75 in)
Description A species commonly observed in large aggregations composed of hundreds of individuals that hover above the branches of coral colonies, where they scamper to hide if threatened. Typical of sheltered waters and lagoons.

Indo-Pacific sergeant
Abudefduf vaigiensis

Range Red Sea, tropical Indo-Pacific
Habitat Coastal waters, shallow reefs, 1–15 m (3–50 ft)
Size Up to 15 cm (6 in)
Description A big and extremely common damselfish in a wide variety of environments, from turbid waters in coastal lagoons to oceanic reef slopes. Strongly social in habit and manifestly territorial, it feeds only on zooplankton and algae.

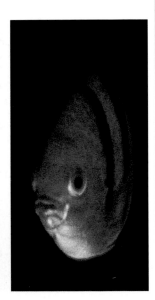

Reticulated dascyllus
Dascyllus reticulatus

Range Tropical Indo-Pacific
Habitat Slopes and outer reefs, 1–50 m (3–165 ft)
Size Up to 6 cm (2.5 in)
Description These little fish live in colonies tied to *Pocillopora* coral, among whose branches they take refuge when frightened. Members of the different *Dascyllus* species—the humbug Dascyllus, *D. aruanus*, and the threespot Dascyllus, *D. trimaculatus,* are also very common—are among the most numerous fish in shallow reef waters. They feed on zooplankton and algae.

Princess damsel
Pomacentrus vaiuli

Range Western Pacific, eastern Indian Ocean
Habitat Coastal waters, outer reefs, 3–25 m (10–80 ft)
Size Up to 8 cm (3 in)
Description A typical pomacentrid with its characteristically polychromatic and fluorescent coloration, common in the most diverse environments of coastal and pelagic reefs but always bound to the seabed.

Jewel damsel
Plectroglyphidodon lacrymatus

135

Range Tropical Indo-Pacific
Habitat Coastal waters, outer reefs, 3–15 m (10–50 ft)
Size Up to 10 cm (4 in)
Description A highly territorial pomacentrid, often aggressive in the face of other species. Rather common on degraded seabeds or where coral formations mix with sandy bottoms and algal meadows. The skin of the young is much more flamboyant than the adults' and is typified by numerous fluorescent blue orbs.

Lemon damsel
Pomacentrus moluccensis

136

Range Western Pacific, eastern Indian Ocean
Habitat Coastal waters, protected reefs, 1–15 m (3–50 ft)
Size Up to 8 cm (3 in)
Description A species characteristic of the most protected seabeds, closely tied to the coral mass and usually observed in small, dispersed groups. It feeds on algae and zooplankton.

Spotted drum
Equetus punctatus

Range Caribbean Sea
Habitat Protected and dimly lit areas of the reef, 1–30 m (3–100 ft)
Size Up to 25 cm (10 in)
Description A species that favors small crevices and the darkest and most protected reef zones; easily identified by the ample growth of the first rays of its dorsal fin (inset photo) and for its curious undulating swim. It is very similar to *E. lanceolatus*.

Dash-and-dot goatfish
Parupeneus barberinus

138

Range Tropical Indo-Pacific
Habitat Coastal reefs and lagoons, 5–100 m (16–330 ft)
Size Up to 40 cm (16 in)
Description A big tropical red mullet, solitary or in small groups, substituted in the Red Sea by the *P. forsskali* species, which it closely resembles. Easily identified by the dot and dash on its body, it can be observed while it rummages on the bottom with its long barbels in search of small crustaceans and invertebrates (for other mullet species, see page 201).

Two-barred goatfish
Parupeneus bifasciatus

139

Range Tropical Indo-Pacific
Habitat Reefs, 1–80 m
(3–260 ft)
Size Up to 30 cm (12 in)
Description A big and generally solitary species often observed as it rests on the tabular formations of *Acropora*. Its coloration is somewhat variable, but it is easy to recognize by two black, highly defined bars on its back. It feeds on small benthic organisms that it catches by violently sifting detritus and sand on the seabed.

113

Blackstriped goatfish
Upeneus tragula

140

Range Tropical Indo-Pacific
Habitat Coastal reefs and lagoons, 3–30 m (10–100 ft)
Size Up to 30 cm (12 in)
Description A rather common species; mullets belong to the goatfish family, represented in tropical seas by about 6 genera and more than 35 species. Generally found in small groups or as isolated exemplars; able to change the chromatic intensity of their skin very rapidly (see page 201 for other mullet species).

Humphead wrasse, napoleonfish *Cheilinus undulatus* 141

Range Red Sea, tropical Indo-Pacific
Habitat Slopes, outer reefs, coral drop-offs, 2–60 m (7–200 ft)
Size Up to 2.3 m (7.5 ft)
Description The biggest member of the labrid family and an extremely odd species. The male adult has a conspicuous bulge on its forehead; it is rather sedentary, and its coloration is very dramatic. Now in grave danger—as are many other coralline fish—because of the strong demand for it in Asian restaurants.

Klunzinger's wrasse
Thalassoma rueppellii 142

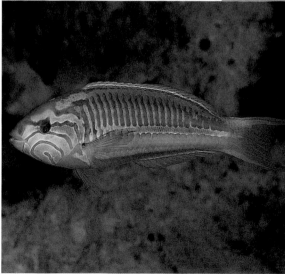

Range Endemic to the Red Sea
Habitat Outer reefs, coral drop-offs, 1–20 m (3–65 ft)
Size Up to 20 cm (8 in)
Description A common species that epitomizes the features of numerous *Thalassoma* tropical species—long, fusiform body, lunate tail, small mouth with sharp teeth, extremely bright coloring, and a "gliding" swim created by the rapid motion of its pectoral fins. Labrids feed mostly on small crustaceans that they capture by rummaging through the sandy seabed.

Bandcheek wrasse
Oxycheilinus digrammus

143

Range Red Sea, tropical Indo-Pacific
Habitat Lagoons and protected seabeds, 3–100 m (10–330 ft)
Size Up to 30 cm (12 in)
Description A typical, mid-size labrid characterized by a bright coloration like its tropical cousins. Rather timid and solitary, it feeds on crustaceans, mollusks and little fish.

Ringtail wrasse
Oxycheilinus unifasciatus

144

Range Tropical Indo-Pacific
Habitat Lagoons, seabeds with coral and detritus, 1–160 m (3–525 ft)
Size Up to 25 cm (10 in)
Description Like almost all other *Oxycheilinus*, this species is an active predator of benthic organisms and also feeds on small fish, crabs, sea urchins and starfish. Like most of its congenerics, it can change its skin color with astonishing speed. Relatively common.

Beaked butterflyfish
Chelmon rostratus

145

Range Western Pacific, Andaman Sea
Habitat Coastal waters, lagoons, estuaries, 1–15 m (3–50 ft)
Size Up to 20 cm (8 in)
Description An elegant species with beautiful silvery scales banded in orange. The black ocellus on its dorsal fin looks like an eye and may confuse its predators. Observed in pairs or alone in lagoons, estuaries, and sometimes in turbid waters on sedimentary bottoms. Locally common but infrequent through its entire range.

Big long-nosed butterflyfish
Forcipiger longirostris

146

Range Tropical Indo-Pacific
Habitat Outer reefs, slopes, 5–60 m (16–200 ft)
Size Up to 22 cm (8.5 in)
Description A highly specialized butterflyfish almost always found in pairs along well-developed reefs, using its long snout to search for small organisms and coral polyps to eat. Timid, approached only with difficulty; sometimes, in some localities, its coloration is entirely brown or black.

Longnose butterflyfish
Forcipiger flavissimus

Range Tropical Indo-Pacific
Habitat Exposed reefs, shallow waters, 2–100 m (7–330 ft)
Size Up to 22 cm (8.5 in)
Description Virtually identical to the preceding species and with the same habits, but differentiated primarily by the lesser development of its snout. It seems to prefer feeding on hydroids, small crustaceans, fish eggs, and the pedicels (or stalks) of sea urchins and starfish.

Panda butterflyfish
Chaetodon adiergastos

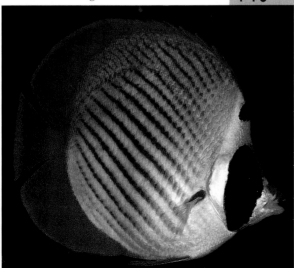

Range Western Pacific Ocean
Habitat Reefs and coral drop-offs, 3–30 m (10–100 ft)
Size Up to 20 cm (8 in)
Description Often in small groups near soft corals or colonies of hydroids. Relatively inactive during the day, it feeds on tiny invertebrates and zooplankton.

Ornate butterflyfish
Chaetodon ornatissimus

Range Andaman Sea, western Pacific Ocean
Habitat Reef margins, coral drop-offs, 1–40 m (3–130 ft)
Size Up to 20 cm (8 in)
Description A species with sedentary habits, observable almost always in pairs near the slopes of seaward reefs. Like the majority of butterflyfish, it uses its highly specialized mouth to suck extended polyps out of stony coral colonies.

Meyer's butterflyfish
Chaetodon meyeri

Range Indian Ocean, western Pacific Ocean
Habitat Outer reefs and lagoons, 5–25 m (16–80 ft)
Size Up to 14 cm (5.5 in)
Description Territorial, almost always in pairs, this species is observable on patches of undisturbed reef. It feeds exclusively on coral polyps, which it plucks out with the help of the rigid bristles that make up its characteristic dentition.

Crown butterflyfish
Chaetodon paucifasciatus

Range Red Sea and Gulf of Aden
Habitat Seabeds with coral and detritus, 4–30 m (13–100 ft)
Size Up to 14 cm (5.5 in)
Description Found in pairs or in small shoals among stony coral formations or in proximity to areas of rubble on the bottom. It feeds on small invertebrates, algae, and the polyps of corals and sea fans.

Redfin butterflyfish
Chaetodon trifasciatus

Range Tropical Indo-Pacific
Habitat Lagoons and coral bottoms, 1–20 m (3–65 ft)
Size Up to 12 cm (4.75 in)
Description Very common in the shallow waters of the reef, on undisturbed seabeds and those rich in coral formations. Usually found in established pairs with territorial behavior. Like all butterflyfish, it feeds on coral polyps.

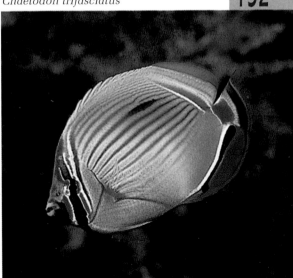

Foureye butterflyfish
Chaetodon capistratus

Range Atlantic Ocean from Massachusetts to the Gulf of Mexico, Caribbean Sea
Habitat Reefs and mixed seabeds, 3–18 m (10–60 ft)
Size Up to 13 cm (5 in)
Description Often in territorial pairs or in small groups spread along the summit of the reef. One of the more common of the twelve *Chaetodon* species found in the tropical Atlantic.

Klein's butterflyfish
Chaetodon kleinii

Range Indian Ocean, western Pacific
Habitat Lagoons and deep seabeds, 10–60 m (33–200 ft)
Size Up to 10 cm (4 in)
Description Characteristic of deep seabeds, often observable on walls or in the channels of atolls, alone or in pairs. Omnivorous, it feeds on coral polyps, algae and zooplankton.

Teardrop butterflyfish
Chaetodon unimaculatus

155

Range Indian Ocean, western Pacific
Habitat Open waters, seaward reef slopes, 1–30 m (3–100 ft)
Size Up to 20 cm (8 in)
Description Common near flats colonized by soft corals of the *Sarcophyton* and *Sinularai* genera. It feeds mostly on coral polyps, polychaetes, crustaceans and filamentous algae. In the western part of its range, it is represented by a totally yellow subspecies.

121

Reticulated butterflyfish
Chaetodon reticulatus

156

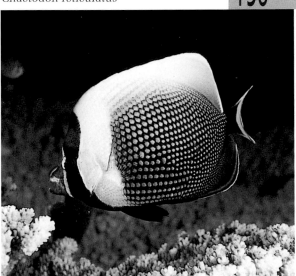

Range Central Indo-Pacific
Habitat Slopes and embankments, 1–30 m (3–100 ft)
Size Up to 13 cm (5 in)
Description Often in pairs, sometimes observed in lagoons where it finds well-developed coral formations. Relatively common in its range of distribution.

Vagabond butterflyfish
Chaetodon vagabundus

157

Range Central Indo-Pacific
Habitat Coastal reefs and lagoons, 1–30 m (3–100 ft)
Size Up to 18 cm (7 in)
Description Often in pairs, a species of large size, common enough in shallow waters. Omnivorous, it feeds on tiny crustaceans, filamentous algae, small invertebrates, coral polyps and worms. As its name implies, it is not territorial and often follows other species.

122

Red Sea raccoon butterflyfish
Chaetodon fasciatus

158

Range Red Sea and Gulf of Aden
Habitat Undisturbed reefs and coral drop-offs, 2–30 m (7–100 ft)
Size Up to 22 cm (8.5 in)
Description Locally very common; observed alone or in pairs, sometimes in small groups. It feeds on tiny crustaceans, coral polyps, hydroids and filamentous algae.

Golden butterflyfish
Chaetodon semilarvatus

Range Endemic to the Red Sea

Habitat Coral flats and drop-offs, 4–20 m (13–65 ft)

Size Up to 23 cm (9 in)

Description Decidedly more nocturnal in behavior than other butterflyfish, it is almost perfectly yellow and round. It can often be approached at close quarters during the day while it hides in crevices or fissures or hovers in small groups in the shelter of large tabular formations of *Acropora* coral. It feeds primarily on coral polyps.

123

Collared butterflyfish
Chaetodon collare

Range Indian Ocean, Andaman Sea
Habitat Outer reefs and slopes, 1–30 m (3–100 ft)
Size Up to 20 cm (8 in)
Description Closely related to the *C. reticulatus*, this species is easily recognized by its pearly gray scales trimmed in gold and its characteristic red caudal peduncle. Often found in shoals that can also be numerous. Omnivorous, it feeds on coral polyps, hydroids and small crustaceans.

124

Raccoon butterflyfish
Chaetodon lunula

Range Tropical Indo-Pacific
Habitat Reefs and slopes, 1–30 m (3–100 ft)
Size Up to 20 cm (8 in)
Description Usually in established pairs, it has sometimes been observed in great shoals in the open ocean (Kuiter/Debelius, 1997). Named for the distinctive black "mask" over its eyes, followed by a white bar. One of the most common of more than 100 *Chaetodon* species that populate seabeds in the tropical Indo-Pacific.

Blackback butterflyfish
Chaetodon melannotus

162

Range Tropical Indo-Pacific
Habitat Coral walls and drop-offs, 1–30 m (3–100 ft)
Size Up to 15 cm (6 in)
Description Often in pairs, sometimes in small, thinly spread groups. Territorial, common among *Acropora* colonies, less specialized diet than other butterflyfish. The name refers to the dorsal area of the body, which turns black.

Humphead bannerfish
Heniochus varius

163

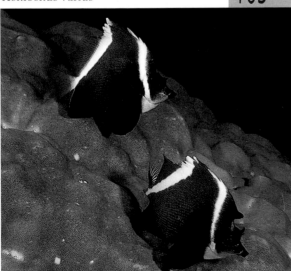

Range Western Pacific Ocean
Habitat Coral slopes and drop-offs, 2–30 m (7–100 ft)
Size Up to 8 inches (20 cm)
Description Often observed in pairs or in small groups in the shelter of ledges or inside caves and fissures, which they rarely leave during the day. The *Heniochus* genus in the chaetodont family is represented by eight species, all of them tropical. The common name refers to the prominent lump on its forehead.

Singular bannerfish
Heniochus singularius

164

Range Eastern Indian Ocean, western Pacific
Habitat Coral slopes and drop-offs, 2–50 m (7–165 ft)
Size Up to 30 cm (12 in)
Description A large species of butterflyfish, observable almost always in pairs, often deep down. This species also favors sheltered places and is often found in cracks or under jutting balconies.

Pennant bannerfish
Heniochus chrysostomus

165

Range Eastern Indian Ocean, western Pacific
Habitat Slopes, lagoons, drop-offs, 1–40 m (3–130 ft)
Size Up to 16 cm (6.25 in)
Description Found in limited groups or more often in couples on slopes, on the rim of embankments and coral drop-offs. Like their congenerics, pennant bannerfish feed on tiny crustaceans, zooplankton and benthic organisms.

Red Sea bannerfish
Heniochus intermedius

166

Range Endemic to the Red Sea
Habitat Outer reefs, coral drop-offs, 3–50 m (10–165 ft)
Size Up to 20 cm (8 in)
Description Almost always in territorial pairs close to coral formations on the seabed, sometimes in small groups. It feeds on benthic invertebrates.

Longfin bannerfish
Heniochus acuminatus

167

Range Tropical Indo-Pacific from Africa to Japan
Habitat Passes, lagoons, seaward reef slopes, 2–70 m (7–230 ft)
Size Up to 20 cm (8 in)
Description Almost always in pairs, it feeds on zooplankton captured in the column of water in front of the coral reef. At first sight, it is hard to distinguish from *H. diphreutes* (page 128) which has, however, different habits and range.

False moorish idol
Heniochus diphreutes

168

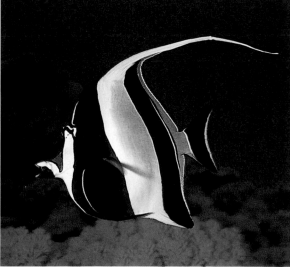

Range Red Sea, Indian Ocean
Habitat Seaward reefs and slopes, 15–200 m (50–660 ft)
Size Up to 20 cm (8 in)
Description Usually in spectacular shoals composed of hundreds or even thousands of individuals suspended in the water column right in front of the reef or in the current at atoll passes. It feeds on zooplankton.

Moorish idol
Zanclus cornutus

169

Range Tropical Indo-Pacific
Habitat Coastal and seaward reefs, 1–180 m (3–590 ft)
Size Up to 22 m (8.5 in)
Description Found alone, in pairs, or in small groups, it is sometimes seen in big shoals; it feeds on algae and small benthic organisms. Its family, the Zanclidae, is closer to surgeonfish (acanthurids) than to butterflyfish (chaetodonts). It is the only member of its species; easily identified by the long dorsal fin ending in a very thin tip.

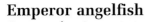

Emperor angelfish
Pomacanthus imperator

Range Red Sea, tropical Indo-Pacific
Habitat Lagoons, walls, coral drop-offs, 2–60 m (7–200 ft)
Size Up to 40 cm (16 in)
Description The pomacanthid family includes some of the most beautiful vari-colored species on the reef. *P. imperator* is often seen in territorial pairs that do not hesitate to confront divers with showy behavior meant to intimidate by producing popping and grumbling sounds easily heard underwater. Family members have a long and pointed preopercular or cheek spine (inset photo) and they feed on sponges, coelenterates and inverte-brates. The coloration of the young (below) is almost always very different from that of adults.

Yellowbar angelfish
Pomacanthus maculosus

Range Red Sea, western Indian Ocean
Habitat Coral drop-offs, 4–12 m (13–40 ft)
Size Up to 50 cm (20 in)
Description A very curious angelfish, it often approaches divers underwater. Beyond being found among coral formations, it also frequents sedimentary bottoms or sometimes turbid waters. Solitary and territorial, it feeds exclusively on sponges and benthic invertebrates.

Semicircle angelfish
Pomacanthus semicirculatus

Range Tropical Indo-Pacific
Habitat Slopes and seaward reefs, 1–40 m (3–130 ft)
Size Up to 35 cm (14 in)
Description Not a common species throughout its broad range, rather cautious and generally hard to approach. Adults are usually observed hiding in cracks or clefts, and most often alone.

Bluering angelfish
Pomacanthus annularis

Range Andaman Sea, Indian Ocean
Habitat Coastal waters, 1–60 m (3–200 ft)
Size Up to 45 cm (18 in)
Description An elegant and unmistakable species, locally common and easily approached in waters that are not necessarily clear; sometimes in areas of rubble, under boulders or even within ports. The adults form stable and sedentary couples that are territorial in behavior.

Six-banded angelfish
Pomacanthus sexstriatus

Range Tropical Indo-Pacific
Habitat Walls and seaward reefs, 5–60 m (16–200 ft)
Size Up to 45 cm (18 in)
Description The coloration of this angelfish is simpler and less dramatic than that of other members of the species. It is usually encountered in stable pairs along slopes or rubbly drop-offs below 20 m (65 ft) in depth. It eats sponges and benthic invertebrates. Rather timid and not especially common.

Blueface angelfish
Pomacanthus xanthometopon

175

Range Eastern Indian Ocean, western Pacific
Habitat Slopes and coral drop-offs, 5–50 m (16–165 ft)
Size Up to 40 cm (16 in)
Description This pomacanthid prefers solitude and exhibits territorial habits. It can be found on seaward reefs and on slopes rich with stony coral formations, cracks and holes. Known for its exceptionally gaudy coloration, it feeds on sponges and benthic invertebrates and is easily approached if one moves cautiously.

132

Gray angelfish
Pomacanthus arcuatus

176

Range Atlantic Ocean from New York to Brazil, Caribbean
Habitat Coral seabeds, algal meadows, 3–25 m (10–80 ft)
Size Up to 60 cm (23 in)
Description Coloration is overall grayish brown, paler at the mouth and with yellow pectorals. Especially majestic in territorial and sedentary pairs as they navigate their turf along the reef. Sometimes it "cleans" larger species. It eats mostly sponges and benthic organisms. Curious and easily approachable.

French angelfish
Pomacanthus paru

177

Range Atlantic Ocean from Florida to Brazil, Caribbean
Habitat Coral drop-offs thick with sponges, 3–25 m (10–80 ft)
Size Up to 45 cm (18 in)
Description Often in pairs on seabeds and walls rich with fissures, gorgonians and sponges, but sometimes near sand flats. When young, it often acts as a "cleaner," feeding on external parasites and shavings of dead skin from larger fish. Although courageous and territorial, it is easy to approach.

Queen angelfish
Holacanthus ciliaris

178

Range Atlantic Ocean from Florida to Brazil, Caribbean
Habitat Coral drop-offs rich in sponges, 6–25 m (20–80 ft)
Size Up to 40 cm (16 in)
Description Superbly colorful in a mixture of blues, greens and yellows. Rather curious, it often approaches divers; it prefers seabeds thick with sea fans, sea whips, and especially sponges, on which it feeds.

King angelfish
Holacanthus passer

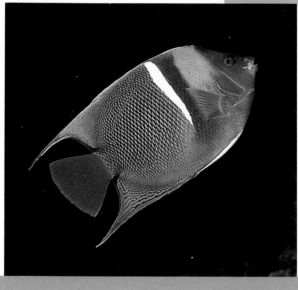

Range Eastern Pacific Ocean from the Gulf of California to Ecuador
Habitat Rocky areas and shallows, 5–50 m (16–165 ft)
Size Up to 40 cm (16 in)
Description This angelfish carries the "cleaner" habits common to its young cousins into adulthood. In some places in the eastern Pacific, it can often be observed feeding on small parasitical crustaceans that infest the skin of scalloped hammerhead sharks, which wait their turn at so-called cleaning stations.

Rock beauty
Holacanthus tricolor

180

Range Atlantic Ocean from Georgia to Brazil, Caribbean
Habitat Coral drop-offs rich in sponges, 3–25 m (10–80 ft)
Size Up to 25 cm (10 in)
Description Extremely territorial, defines precisely the areas that it patrols. Relatively curious, it sometimes lingers to watch divers and strikes a menacing posture by presenting its flank. Its yellow front body and tail with black rear body are unmistakable. It feeds mostly on sponges and benthic invertebrates.

Regal angelfish
Pygoplites diacanthus

Range Red Sea, tropical Indo-Pacific
Habitat Undisturbed reefs, 2–80 m (7–260 ft)
Size Up to 25 cm (10 in)
Description A very elegant species, fairly common on undisturbed barriers with abundant madreporic formations, it is often bound to the microenvironment of coral colonies among whose branches it finds easy refuge. Rather shy, it can sometimes be observed in aberrant colorations differentiated by the shape of its stripes. It eats sponges and invertebrates.

Threespot angelfish
Apolemichthys trimaculatus

Range Tropical Indo-Pacific
Habitat Rubble seabeds, reefs rich with sponges and soft corals, 3–60 m (10–200 ft)
Size Up to 26 cm (10 in)
Description This angelfish finds its favorite habitat in stretches of barrier reef or isolated formations rich with sponges, whip corals or soft corals. Sometimes observed in small, wide-ranging groups.

Latticed sandperch
Parapercis clathrata

Range Central Indo-Pacific
Habitat Sandy bottoms and areas of rubble, 2–15 m (7–50 ft)
Size Up to 25 cm (10 in)
Description Observed near slopes on seabeds with detritus or on sandy flats in the reef while it rests on the seabed, characteristically perched on its pectoral fins. A relatively active species but easily approached.

Speckled sandperch
Parapercis hexophthalma

Range Red Sea, Indo-Pacific
Habitat Sandy bottoms and areas of rubble, 2–22 m (7–72 ft)
Size Up to 26 cm (10 in)
Description Easily observed near rubbly and sandy seabeds or among coral formations on the reef; sometimes in pairs but more often alone. Sandperch are equipped with strong teeth, and they feed on small fish and invertebrates that they capture in speedy bursts.

Pictus blenny
Ecsenius pictus

Range Central Indo-Pacific
Habitat Coral drop-offs, 15–40 m (50–130 ft)
Size Up to 4.5 cm (1.75 in)
Description A small blenny frequently seen on exposed perches on coral or sponges, alone or in pairs. Highly territorial but timid and hard to approach.

Linear blenny
Ecsenius lineatus

Range Indian Ocean
Habitat Coral drop-offs, 1–30 m (3–100 ft)
Size Up to 4 cm (1.5 in)
Description A small blenny observed alone or in pairs, generally on very exposed perches but always ready to hide in one of the narrow cracks it adopts as its burrow.

THE REEF COMMUNITY

Bath's comb-tooth
Ecsenius bathi

Range Central Indo-Pacific
Habitat Slopes and coral drop-offs, 3–30 m (10–100 ft)
Size Up to 4 cm (1.5 in)
Description A small blenny characteristic of seabeds rich with coral and generally observed on exposed perches such as sponges or corals. If threatened, it darts off like lightning and quickly perches a short distance away.

138

Bluestriped fangblenny
Plagiotremus rhinorhynchus

188

Range Red Sea, tropical Indo-Pacific
Habitat Coral drop-offs, 0.5–3 m (1.5–10 ft)
Size Up to 10 cm (4 in)
Description A small, lean blenny with a vividly colored skin, always ready to dart into one of the small cracks it always stays near. The young are aggressive mimics of the *Labroides dimidiatus* cleaner fish, but the adults eventually feed only on zooplankton.

Mandarinfish
Synchiropus splendidus

189

Range Central Indo-Pacific
Habitat Seabeds with detritus, 1–30 m (3–100 ft)
Size Up to 6 cm (2.5 in)
Description Members of the Callionymidae family never leave the sea bottom where they hop among the fragments of dead coral that are their favorite habitat. The mandarinfish is locally widespread but, despite its splendid coloration, it is generally difficult to observe. The family it belongs to contains at least nine genera and about 125 different species.

Fingered dragonet
Dactylopus dactylopus

190

Range Central Indo-Pacific
Habitat Sedimentary and sandy seabeds, 1–50 m (3–165 ft)
Size Up to 18 cm (7 in)
Description Easily identified by a splendid dorsal fin that is immediately unfolded in case of danger. May sometimes be seen as it moves around on a muddy sea floor with an assist from its pectoral fins. The immature specimen in the small photo is only a few millimeters long.

Striped triplefin
Helcogramma striatum

Range Tropical Indo-Pacific
Habitat Sponges and corals, 6–30 m (20–100 ft)
Size Up to 4 cm (1.5 in)
Description The helcogrammas are similar to tiny blennies. They can be observed while perched on their pectorals in wide-open positions on the surface of sponges or corals. *H. striatum* is perhaps the most easily identified among more than 200 species belonging to the Tripterygiidae (three-finned) family thanks to its bright fluorescent colors.

Gobies
Trimma sp.

Range Tropical Indo-Pacific
Habitat Sponges and soft corals, 1–70 m (3–230 ft)
Size Up to 2 cm (0.75 in)
Description Among salt-water fish families, gobies claim the most genera (more than 200) and the most species (more than 500 in the Indo-Pacific alone). Members of the *Trimma* genus almost always perch on soft corals and sponges and reside there, demarcating a territory from which they never stray. They feed on tiny crustaceans and zoo-plankton.

Peppermint goby
Coryphopterus lipernes

Range Florida, Caribbean Sea
Habitat Coral drop-offs, 10–40 m (33–130 ft)
Size Up to 3 cm (1.25 in)
Description This small Caribbean goby is easily approached and recognized by its golden color on a translucent background and by the fluorescent blue markings on its head. It is a sedentary and territorial species that usually perches on a coral head; eats zooplankton and tiny benthic crustaceans.

Gobies
Eviota sp.

Range Tropical Indo-Pacific
Habitat Coral seabeds, 1–30 m (3–100 ft)
Size Up to 2.5 cm (1 in)
Description The *Eviota* genus is made up of numerous species that cannot easily be differentiated without a microscopic examination. Most are tiny, territorial and semi-transparent gobies, and can often be seen on the surface of sponges and soft corals where they stake out well-defined territories.

Crab-eye goby
Signigobius biocellatus

Range Western Pacific Ocean
Habitat Sandy and rubbly seabeds, 2–30 m (7–100 ft)
Size Up to 10 cm (4 in)
Description This species has extremely interesting habits. It forms stable, territorial pairs that are easily approached while they busily filter mouthfuls of sand in the immediate vicinity of their burrow. If alarmed, these little gobies raise their showy dorsal fins decorated with ocelli, simulate crablike lateral movements, and move away by hops.

Fire dartfish
Nemateleotris magnifica

Range Tropical Indo-Pacific
Habitat Coral drop-offs, 6–50 m (20–165 ft)
Size Up to 7.5 cm (3 in)
Description This fish is immediately identifiable by the yellowish color on its front half and red in the back, and by its habit of resting suspended above the burrow it digs into the substrate, into which it disappears in a flash when it feels threatened. Almost always in stable pairs, it can sometimes be found in collections of individuals of different ages; it feeds on zooplankton.

Decorated dartfish
Nemateleotris decora

197

Range Central Indo-Pacific
Habitat Rocky bottoms and drop-offs, 20–70 m (65–230 ft)
Size Up to 7.5 cm (3 in)
Description Its habits are similar to those of the preceding species, which it generally trades places with at depths of 30 m (100 ft) and beyond. Usually in pairs suspended over a burrow dug out of the substrate; it is extremely timid and hard to approach.

Blackfin dartfish
Ptereleotris evides

198

Range Indian Ocean, western Pacific Ocean
Habitat Seabeds with detritus or mixed materials, 3–50 m (10–165 ft)
Size Up to 12 cm (4.75 in)
Description Habitually found in pairs suspended in the water column a little above their burrow dug into the substrate, where it disappears with a lightning-fast spurt if disturbed. It eats zooplankton exclusively

Spotted prawn-goby
Amblyeleotris guttata

Range Western and central Pacific Ocean
Habitat Sand and rubble bottoms, 10–35 m (33–115 ft)
Size Up to 7 cm (2.75 in)
Description Especially showy coloration and often found in the company of one or more alpheid shrimps. Like all its cousins, it communicates with the virtually blind symbiont shrimp through vibrations conveyed by its tail fin, which is always in contact with the body of the tiny crustacean.

144

Banded or yellow prawn-goby
Cryptocentrus cinctus

Range Western Pacific Ocean
Habitat Sedimentary and sandy seabeds, 1–15 m (3–50 ft)
Size Up to 6 cm (2.5 in)
Description Characteristic of silted bottoms and calm waters, known to have two distinct color phases: brown bands (inset photo) or entirely chromium yellow, sometimes classified as *C. cinctus flavus*. Locally abundant and territorial.

Gorgeous prawn-goby
Amblyeleotris wheeleri

201

Range Tropical Indo-Pacific
Habitat Areas of detritus and sandy bottoms, 5–15 m (16–50 ft)
Size Up to 6.5 cm (2.5 in)
Description Observed on sandy, rubbly, and often volcanic seabeds, generally accompanying one or more blind alpheid shrimps with which it shares a burrow dug into the substrate. Like all symbiont gobies, it is very shy and always ready to disappear rapidly into its burrow.

Metallic prawn-goby
Amblyeleotris latifasciata

202

Range Borneo, Indonesia
Habitat Sandy seabeds, 10–40 m (33–130 ft)
Size Up to 14 cm (5.5 in)
Description Usually solitary, this beautiful goby is often observable in the company of one or more shrimps of the *Alpheus* genus with which it shares a burrow dug into the sandy substrate. It can easily be identified by the iridescent speckles that stud its coat.

Steinitz's prawn-goby
Amblyeleotris steinitzi

Range Red Sea, tropical Indo-Pacific
Habitat Sandy and pebbled seabeds, 6–30 m (20–100 ft)
Size Up to 8 cm (3 in)
Description A small goby that shares its burrow in the sandy substrate with the *Alpheus djeddensis* shrimp. Like its cousins, it is markedly territorial and very attentive to everything that happens in its immediate surroundings.

Filament-finned prawn-goby
Stonogobiops nematodes

Range Central Indo-Pacific
Habitat Pebbled and sandy seabeds, 8–40 m (26–130 ft)
Size Up to 6 cm (2.5 in)
Description Easily identified at first glance by a coat crossed with wide black and white bands, almost always in pairs above the burrow dug into the substrate that it shares with the *Alpheus randalli* shrimp. Very diffident and approachable only with great difficulty.

Maiden goby
Valenciennea puellaris

205

Range Tropical Indo-Pacific, subtropical waters
Habitat Sandy bottoms and mixed reefs, 3–25 m (10–80 ft)
Size Up to 14 cm (5.5 in)
Description Generally found in pairs near its burrow dug into the substrate. More easily approachable than other species and immediately recognizable by its vivid orange spots. Reaches bigger sizes in subtropical waters.

THE REEF COMMUNITY

147

Longspine goby
Coryphopterus longispinus

206

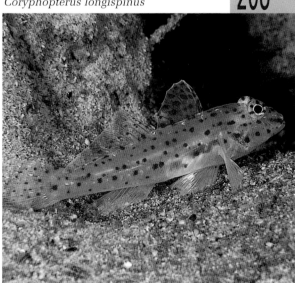

Range Red Sea, tropical Indo-Pacific
Habitat Areas of rubble on the seabed, 9–18 m (30–60 ft)
Size Up to 6 cm (2.5 in)
Description Identifiable by its triangular head and a semi-transparent body decorated with oval spots in a vivid orange color. A species with typically sedentary habits, easily observed on sandy bottoms in front of crevices, and on rubbly terraces on walls.

Longnose filefish
Oxymonocanthus longirostris

207

Range Tropical Indo-Pacific
Habitat Coastal waters, 0.5–35 m (1.5–115 ft)
Size Up to 10 cm (4 in)
Description This brilliantly colored species is intimately bound to the microenvironment provided by the oldest *Acropora* colonies. Adults generally swim in stable pairs while juveniles appear more often in groups. They both continually weave among the branches of stony coral colonies, grazing on any extended polyps.

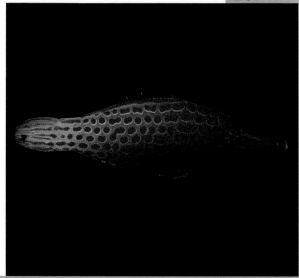

148

Blacksaddle mimic
Paraluteres prionurus

208

Range Tropical Indo-Pacific
Habitat Coastal reefs, 1–25 m (3–80 ft)
Size Up to 10 cm (4 in)
Description This small monacanthid ably exploits its close resemblance to the poisonous black-saddled toby, *Canthigaster valentini* (see page 154) by imitating its coloration to perfection and sharing its habitat as well. It is often observed in small scattered groups.

Scrawled filefish
Aluterus scriptus

Range Cosmopolitan in tropical and subtropical seas
Habitat Coastal waters, 2–80 m (7–260 ft)
Size Up to 1.1 m (3.5 ft)
Description Unmistakable species with awkward posture and a long broomlike tail. Solitary and very agile. Assumes a well-camouflaged coloration while reclining on one flank among the corals (inset photo).

Yellowmargin triggerfish
Pseudobalistes flavomarginatus

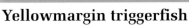

Range Tropical Indo-Pacific
Habitat Coastal waters, 2–50 m (7–165 ft)
Size Up to 60 cm (23 in)
Description Quite similar to the *Balistoides viridescens* species (see page 150) but much less aggressive. Generally solitary, sometimes found in loose groups in shared localities during the mating season. Active, robust and curious like all of its congenerics, able to swim very fast for short stretches. It feeds on crustaceans and echinoderms.

Mustache triggerfish
Balistoides viridescens

Range Tropical Indo-Pacific, Red Sea
Habitat Coastal waters, 5–35 m (16–115 ft)
Size Up to 75 cm (29 in)
Description The biggest and most robust triggerfish, it is extremely aggressive toward divers during the mating season or when standing guard near its nest. Able to inflict deep, painful bites with strong teeth capable of penetrating metal. A wound from this balistid can even require several stitches. Immediately recognizable by its rather dull, yellowish-green color braided with darker tonalities. It is widespread and we strongly advise divers to avoid encroaching on its territory underwater. Triggerfish define their territories as an area that extends from the seabed to the surface of the water, and divers do well to cut a wide swath around it. This species is fast and bold and does not hesitate to chase presumed intruders over long distances. It feeds chiefly on echinoderms, crustaceans and bivalves.

Orangestriped triggerfish

Balistapus undulatus

Range Tropical Indo-Pacific, Red Sea
Habitat Coastal waters, 2–50 m (7–165 ft)
Size Up to 30 cm (12 in)
Description Common in mixed environments and places rich with invertebrates in which the coral is mixed with sponges; it feeds principally on crustaceans and echinoderms. Its gaudy greenish coloration striped diagonally in orange is unmistakable; it has a yellow tail and its chin and lips are blue. In general, it is a relatively cautious species, rated highly by aquarists.

T H E   R E E F   C O M M U N I T Y

Blue or rippled triggerfish

Pseudobalistes fuscus

Range Tropical Indo-Pacific, Red Sea
Habitat Coastal waters, shallows in the open, 3–50 m (10–165 ft)
Size Up to 55 cm (22 in)
Description Often seen on sand flats and rubbly ledges at the base of the reef, where it searches for prey by blowing into the sandy bottom. The blue coloration is characteristic of adult males and the tonality intensifies during the mating season; in younger individuals the brighter base color is yellow with countless irregular azure streaks.

Range Tropical Indo-Pacific, Red Sea
Habitat Coastal waters, 5–60 m (16–200 ft)
Size Up to 35 cm (14 in)
Description Probably one of the most flamboyant species in tropical seas, with an absolutely unique coloration. It is a very active triggerfish, easy to find near slopes and along the deepest drop-offs. It feeds chiefly on crustaceans and echinoderms, which it easily devours with its strong teeth. The photo at right shows a very young specimen, just two centimeters long, whose costume is strikingly different from that of the adult.

Redtooth triggerfish
Odonus niger

Range Red Sea, tropical Indo-Pacific
Habitat Open waters and seaward reef, 2–35 m (7–115 ft)
Size Up to 35 cm (14 in)
Description Social, it gathers in great shoals to hunt zooplankton and is recognized by its velvety blue-violet colors, lunate tail with elongated lobes, a deep and compressed body, and protruding red teeth. If threatened, it quickly darts into a hole in the seabed, leaving only its tail sticking out.

Black triggerfish
Melichthys niger

215

Range Circumtropical
Habitat Open waters, shallows, exposed reefs, 5–35 m (16–115 ft)
Size Up to 25 cm (10 in)
Description Typical of deep rocky bottoms, open waters, exposed reefs with strong currents, or in the movement of the surf. Very similar to its cousin *M. indicus*, whose range is limited to the Indian Ocean; the difference between them is the absence of a white margin on the tail. A pelagic species, it normally lives in large shoals composed of hundreds of individuals.

Black-saddled toby
Canthigaster valentini

Range Tropical Indo-Pacific
Habitat Coastal reefs, 1–30 m (3–100 ft)
Size Up to 10 cm (4 in)
Description A small puffer fish with a long, pointed snout and toxic flesh, whose appearance is imitated by the blacksaddle mimic, *Paraluteres prionurus* (see page 148). Common enough, it is easily observed on coral drop-offs or near slopes as it swims stiffly with a rapid beating of its pectoral fins.

Spotted toby
Canthigaster solandri

Range Tropical Indo-Pacific
Habitat Slopes, walls full of crevices, 2–50 m (7–165 ft)
Size Up to 10 cm (4 in)
Description A small and intensely colored puffer that is fairly common along embankments and walls rich with fissures and shadowy hollows. Very similar in aspect and behavior to *C. papua*; the range of the two species overlaps in many places. Sometimes confused with *C. compressa*, which is limited to granular or sedimentary seabeds. The flesh of all tetraodontids is highly toxic.

Whitespotted puffer
Arothron hispidus

219

Range Red Sea, tropical Indo-Pacific
Habitat Coral seabeds or mixed materials, 1–30 m (3–100 ft)
Size Up to 50 cm (20 in)
Description Relatively common in various environments, as often on the reef as in seagrass flats or estuarine beds. Like all puffers, it can inflate itself to twice its normal size by swallowing water or air when threatened. It feeds on benthic invertebrates and especially echinoderms, which it chews up easily with its strong, beaklike teeth.

THE REEF COMMUNITY

155

Map puffer
Arothron mappa

220

Range Tropical Indo-Pacific
Habitat Coastal reefs and coral drop-offs, 5–30 m (16–100 ft)
Size Up to 60 cm (23 in)
Description A big, solitary and uncommon species sometimes observed at rest in the shelter of large tabular *Acropora* coral formations or in caves. Its coloration is quite variable, but often characterized by a tangle of thin white strips on a grayish blue ground. If bothered, it can inflict serious wounds with its strong teeth.

Star puffer
Arothron stellatus

221

Range Tropical Indo-Pacific
Habitat Coastal reefs, rubbly seabeds, 3–60 m (10–200 ft)
Size Up to 1.2 m (4 ft)
Description This large species is generally solitary and can often be observed resting in the shelter of projecting ledges and in caves. Like all puffers, it feeds on crustaceans and echinoderms; it cracks open their shells with its powerful jaws, wherein the teeth are fused to form four plates, two in each jaw (the family name Tetradontidae means "four tooth").

Striped puffer
Arothron manilensis

222

Range Central Indo-Pacific
Habitat Sedimentary seabeds, 1–25 m (3–80 ft)
Size Up to 30 cm (12 in)
Description A typical inhabitant of sedimentary and sandy seabeds, it is occasionally found in turbid or salty waters and near estuaries. Often in small dispersed groups, motionless on the bottom, it is recognizable by longitudinal stripes on the yellowish background. Like all puffers, it can inflate itself with water or air if frightened, although in doing so, it risks serious wounds.

Blackspotted puffer
Arothron nigropunctatus

Range Tropical Indo-Pacific
Habitat Coral seabeds, 3–25 m (10–80 ft)
Size Up to 30 cm (12 in)
Description By far the most common species on completely coralline seabeds, often observable during the night while it rests in the hollows of giant barrel sponges of the *Xestospongia* genus. This puffer—whose flesh is as toxic as any of its congenerics—is distinguished by a highly variable coloration. Most of the time it is gray or hazelnut, but is also often seen in glowing yellow and even powder blue. It can puff up with water or air if frightened.

Black-blotched porcupinefish
Diodon liturosus

224

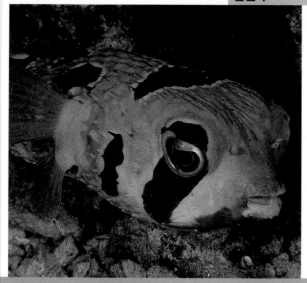

Range Tropical Indo-Pacific
Habitat Coastal reefs, 1–90 m (3–295 ft)
Size Up to 45 cm (18 in)
Description Closely related to puffers, porcupinefish are additionally furnished with scales modified into long, sharp spines that stand up and out when the animal inflates itself. Like puffers, its fused teeth form a powerful structure similar to a beak, which enables it to break open the shells of echinoderms, mollusks and crustaceans.

Bridled burrfish
Chilomycterus antennatus

225

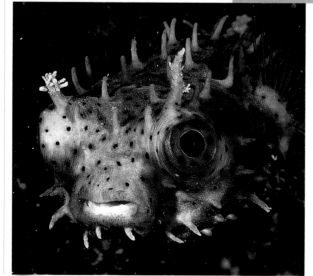

Range Tropical Atlantic Ocean, Caribbean Sea
Habitat Coral drop-offs, 1–30 m (3–100 ft)
Size Up to 30 cm (12 in)
Description A rare species, observable only occasionally near the seabed along coral drop-offs or on seagrass meadows. Wary and hard to approach; the young are a few centimeters long and vivid yellow. At least four other species of porcupinefish in the *Diodon* and *Chilomycterus* genera are found in the Caribbean.

Yellow boxfish
Ostracion cubicus

 226

Range Red Sea, tropical Indo-Pacific
Habitat Coral drop-offs and lagoons, 1–35 m (3–115 ft)
Size Up to 45 cm (18 in)
Description One of the more common species in the boxfish or trunkfish family, the members of this species are characterized by a body encased in a shell of bony hexagonal plates. Some species of Ostraciidae secrete a skin mucus that is especially toxic to other fish. This and similar species feed mostly on algae and small benthic organisms.

Spotted trunkfish
Ostracion meleagris

227

Range Tropical Indo-Pacific
Habitat Coral seabeds, 3–40 m (10–130 ft)
Size Up to 20 cm (8 in)
Description A small and very wary species, the males brandish an extraordinary coloration with few equals in the underwater world. Like all trunkfish, it swims awkwardly but succeeds in moving easily through the coral maze. If threatened, it secretes a toxic mucus all over its body.

NUDIBRANCHS

It is obvious why nudibranchs (sea slugs) are known by their popular name of "jewels of the sea." They are considered by many as the most beautiful marine animal, but they are actually close relatives of the less spectacular and more familiar snails. Deprived of their cousins' protective shells, these fascinating mollusk gastropods have evolved a series of complex and sophisticated defensive systems whose broad efficacy is usually announced clearly to potential predators by an "aposematic" or cautionary coloration that has no true equal in the world of the reef. Though exceptionally diverse in color and shape, all nudibranchs share a muscular foot that allows them to crawl along the bottom. They have a highly abrasive tongue called a radula, a pair of sensory organs on the "forehead" called rhinophores and, as a general rule, a completely bare, external branchlike apparatus on the dorsal surface (thus the name nudibranchs meaning "naked branchia").

These mollusks are carnivorous and predatory, and many fend off enemies by manufacturing their own toxins or acids. Others absorb the stinging cells produced by their customary prey, such as hydroids or sea anemones without discharging them, changing them into defensive weapons. Ironically, their

1. *Hexabranchus sanguineus*
Range Red Sea, tropical Indo-Pacific

2. *Chromodoris quadricolor*
Range Tropical Indo-Pacific

3. *Nembrotha lineolata*
Range Tropical Indo-Pacific

4. *Nembrotha kubaryana*
Range Tropical Indo-Pacific

5. *Nembrotha* sp.
Range Central Indo-Pacific

6. *Roboastra arika*
Range Tropical Indo-Pacific

7. *Tambja morosa*
Range Tropical Indo-Pacific

8. *Chromodoris geminus*
Range Red Sea, tropical Indo-Pacific

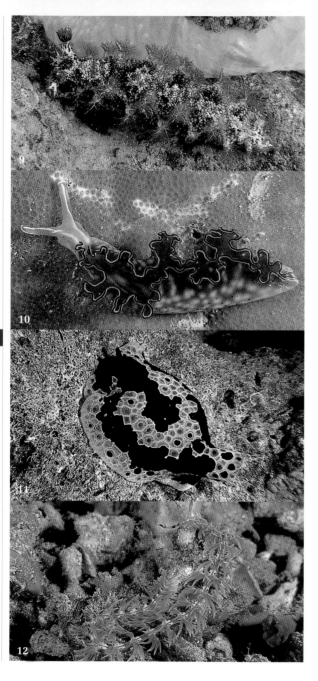

most feared enemies belong to their own family; beyond feeding on sponges and hydroids, many sea slugs actively prey on other nudibranchs.

Nudibranchs are hermaphrodites; every individual exhibits male and female sexual organs and is thus able to couple with any other individual of the same species. It is not uncommon to see the delicate "wreaths" of eggs deposited like multicolored lacework among reef corals by these gastropods. Nudibranchs range in size from a few millimeters (fractions of an inch) to more than 50 cm (20 in). (A "monster" of this size that was probably a member of the *Hexabranchus* genus was recently observed and photographed near Djibouti in the southern Red Sea); in the great majority of cases, however, they vary between 4 to 10 cm (1.5 to 4 in). The most famous of the larger species is surely the so-called Spanish dancer, *Hexabranchus sanguineus*. It is generally bright scarlet in color and nicknamed for the supple undulating motions it uses to move in open water. The symbiont shrimp *Periclemenes imperator* is often observed in the shelter of the dancer's gill tufts, where it feeds on its host's excrement.

Nudibranchs can generally be found during the day in a great variety of environments, mostly in reef zones with the most sponges. Their distribution is circumtropical, but the majority of

9. *Marionia* sp.
Range Tropical Indo-Pacific

10. *Elysia ornata*
Range Tropical Indo-Pacific

11. *Pleurobranchus grandis*
Range Red Sea, tropical Indo-Pacific

12. *Pteraeolidia ianthina*
Range Tropical Indo-Pacific

13. *Phyllidia varicosa*
Range Red Sea, tropical Indo-Pacific

14. *Chromodoris leopardus*
Range Tropical Indo-Pacific

15. *Phyllidia ocellata*
Range Red Sea, tropical Indo-Pacific

16. *Phyllidiopsis fissurtus*
Range Tropical Indo-Pacific

species are found in the central Indo-Pacific basin. Many of them have yet to be classified decisively; indeed, there are common and even conspicuous local variations in skin color and design within the same species.

17. *Chromodoris annae*
Range Tropical Indo-Pacific

18. *Hypselodoris bullocki*
Range Tropical Indo-Pacific

19. *Risbecia pulchella*
Range Red Sea, tropical Indo-Pacific

20. *Chromodoris kuniei*
Range Tropical Indo-Pacific

21. *Halgerda malesso*
Range Tropical Indo-Pacific

22. *Chromodoris reticulata*
Range Tropical Indo-Pacific

23. *Chromodoris coi*
Range Tropical Indo-Pacific

24. *Glossodoris cincta*
Range Red Sea, tropical Indo-Pacific

Nudibranchs

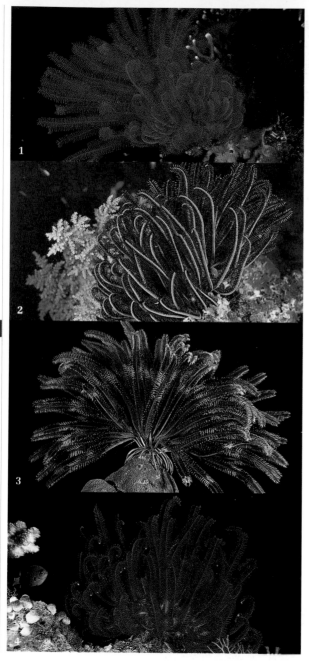

CRINOIDS

Crinoids, or sea lilies and feather stars, are echinoderms with ancient origins and with two series of limbs. The lower, smaller ones are used to grip the gorgonian and coral branches where crinoids settle at night, while the much larger upper limbs are used to perambulate or to filter the zooplankton that these invertebrates eat. Most crinoids remain permanently attached to the bottom. If the animal is forced from the substrate, the upper limbs can be used to "swim" with a movement that is as elegant as it is inefficient. The pentagonal symmetry of echinoderms is visible in the number of crinoid arms, which is generally a multiple of five. Most species have from ten to thirty, but some have more than a hundred. Every arm has a series of minute lateral branches (called pinnules or branchlets), derived from an evolutionary modification of the ambulacral pedicels found on sea urchins and starfish, which transform them into a highly efficient filtering instrument. The plankton is captured and passed from branchlet to branchlet until it reaches the crinoid's mouth, which is situated on the animal's dorsal side—unlike its location on urchins and starfish. These are nocturnal animals that grip the top of gorgonians and corals in places that are hammered by currents where

they can carry out their filtering activity. Various symbiotic species find refuge in the tangle of crinoid arms; the best known are the *Periclemenes ceratophthalmus* prawn (see page 254), the crinoid squat lobster, *Allogalathea elegans* (see page 253), and fish of the genus *Discotrema*.

1. Comantheria schlegeli
Range Central Indo-Pacific

2. Comantheria briareus
Range Central Indo-Pacific

3. Oxycomanthus bennetti
Range Central Indo-Pacific

4. Comantheria sp.
Range Central Indo-Pacific

5. Discotrema sp.
Range Central Indo-Pacific

6. Allogalathea elegans
Range Tropical Indo-Pacific

7. Periclemenes sp.
Range Tropical Indo-Pacific

8. Periclemenes sp.
Range Tropical Indo-Pacific

Crinoids

STARFISH

The echinoderm class comprises more than six thousand different species, all of them marine—not many, if you compare them to crustaceans or mollusks, but all of them unquestionably successful. In practice, echinoderms have colonized every type of submarine environment. Sea stars (starfish), brittle stars, sea urchins, crinoids (feather stars, sea lilies), and holothurians (sea cucumbers) are in this group. Though these animals seem to have little in common with one another, they obviously share symmetrically structured, pentagonal bodies as well as an external skeleton of calcareous plates located just beneath their skin. The animals' characteristic tube feet project from these plates, which take their most sophisticated form in the urchins' spikes (echinoderm in fact means "spiny skin"). Another trait common to all echinoderms is their hydraulic or water-vascular system of movement in which sea water is circulated through their bodies to their tube feet. In this way starfish, urchins and brittle stars move along the bottom and procure food.

Starfish are probably the easiest echinoderms to recognize. They are predatory animals (feeding mostly on bivalve mollusks) and can evert the stomach outside the body to ingest and partly digest

1. *Fromia monilis*
Range Tropical Indo-Pacific

2. *Fromia nodosa*
Range Tropical Indo-Pacific

3. *Fromia milleporella*
Range Red Sea, tropical Indo-Pacific

4. *Choriaster granulatus*
Range Tropical Indo-Pacific

5. *Culcita novaeguineae*
Range Andaman Sea, western Pacific

6. *Acanthaster planci*
Range Tropical Indo-Pacific, eastern Pacific

7. *Oreaster occidentalis*
Range Eastern Pacific Ocean from Baja California to Peru

8. *Protoreaster nodosus*
Range Tropical Indo-Pacific

Starfish

their prey. Their tube feet have suction cups that allow them to move in any direction. Some species, like the feared *Acanthaster planci* or crown-of-thorns star, have specialized diets. *Acanthaster* feeds exclusively on coral polyps and is able to wreak serious damage on the ecosystem of a reef if its numbers are not kept under control by the predation of its natural enemy, the trumpet triton, *Charonia tritonis* (see page 269). The starfish—and their closest relatives, the brittle stars— are nocturnal animals that pass the hours of light in the shelter of fissures and small cavities or under blocks of dead coral. Despite their natural defenses (sensory tentacles and spines, sometimes covered with toxic mucus) and their tough bodies, they are actually a desirable prey. If an individual is not too damaged, it can usually regenerate an amputated limb, just as a limb can regenerate a complete individual. Sometimes both the dorsal and ventral sides of several species host various symbionts. In the most common instance, the cushion star, *Culcita novaeguineae,* will often be easy to find on the *Periclemenes soror* shrimp.

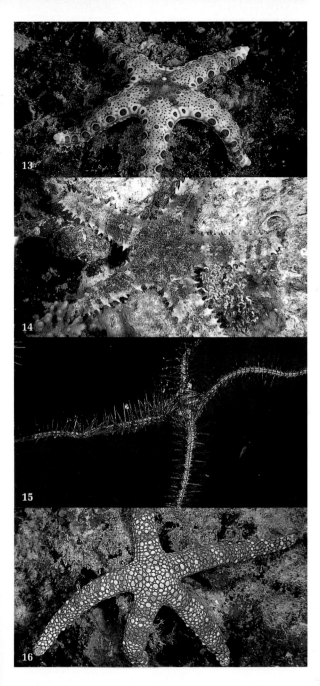

9. *Linckia laevigata*
Range Tropical Indo-
Pacific

10. *Linckia multifora*
Range Red Sea, tropical
Indo-Pacific

11. *Gomophia egyptiaca*
Range Red Sea, tropical
Indo-Pacific

12. *Echinaster callosus*
Range Red Sea, tropical
Indo-Pacific

13. *Neoferdina
glyptodisca*
Range Central Indo-
Pacific

14. *Astropecten* sp.
Range Circumtropical

15. *Ophiotrix* sp.
Range Circumtropical

16. *Nardoa frianti*
Range Central Indo-
Pacific

Starfish

PHYTOPHAGES

Parrotfish (below) and surgeon-fish (facing page) have various traits in common with herbi-vores on land; the former modify their territory; the latter live in "herds" composed of hundreds of individuals.

Preceding pages: Parrotfish, Red Sea

THE REEF'S GREEN PASTURES

Among the reef's inhabitants are the phytophages—herbivores or plant-eaters—who nevertheless occasionally eat live prey. In fact, various species are highly evolved in this direction and have developed sophisticated adaptations of their chewing apparatus along with special behaviors to better exploit their ecological niche. Like many plant-eaters on land, reef herbi-vores tend to gather in herds and change the appearance of their territory through their feeding behavior. Not all these species behave the same, however, even though their actions seem compa-rable. Although they are easily observed as they continuously "graze" coral summits, butterfly-fish or chaetodonts are essential-ly carnivores, despite appear-ances. Using teeth composed of rigid bristles and a tweezer-like mouth apparatus, they can pluck polyps out of stony coral colonies without damaging them. The larg-

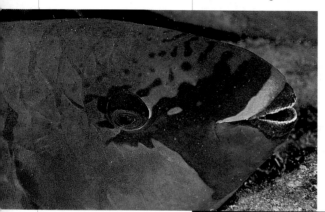

Members of the Scaridae and Acanthuridae families often display surprisingly ornate and beautiful colors. Few fish can match the polychromes of the Cetoscarus bicolor *parrotfish (right) or the male surgeonfish,* Naso vlamingii, *during mating season (below).*

er angelfish or pomacanthids do much the same to sponges and coelenterates. The surgeonfish or acanthurids use very similar teeth, which look like toothbrushes, to efficiently scrape large quantities of encrusted green algae off coral formations, thereby competing with far smaller and less efficient herbivores, such as some species of gobies and blennies. Damselfish or pomacentrids are small, sedentary fish that actively cultivate and defend their own personal "plot" of algae. Different but just as fascinating are parrotfish or scarids, whose teeth are fused into a very strong "beak" composed of two upper and two lower plates. Thanks to their evolved dental apparatus—integrated with powerful and bony pharyngeal plaques—the scarids are capable of crunching and crumbling whole fragments of coral. Once the algae within the coral scraps are digested, everything else is expelled from the intestine in the form of very fine sand. It has been calculated that a population of parrotfish can produce up to a ton of coral sand for every hectare (2.5 acres) per year, which probably makes scarids—along with sea urchins, who are also intensely efficient algae scrapers—the chief modifiers of the reef ecosystem.

Power in Numbers
Pomacentrids or damselfish are small, sedentary, herbivorous fish that are powerless to resist the surgeonfish that attack in shoals by the hundreds. Damselfish demonstrate aggression toward other herbivorous species, but are defeated in this case by sheer numbers (for other advantages offered by "group strategies" see the chapter starting on page 192).

PARROTFISH

Belonging to the scarid family, parrotfish or pollyfish are among the reef's most conspicuous inhabitants. They are closely related to labrids and, like them, are distinguished by a bright coloration that mutates radically

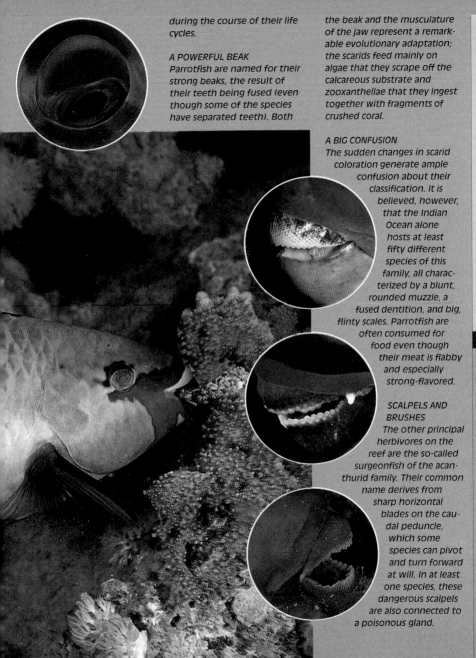

during the course of their life cycles.

A POWERFUL BEAK
Parrotfish are named for their strong beaks, the result of their teeth being fused (even though some of the species have separated teeth). Both the beak and the musculature of the jaw represent a remarkable evolutionary adaptation; the scarids feed mainly on algae that they scrape off the calcareous substrate and zooxanthellae that they ingest together with fragments of crushed coral.

A BIG CONFUSION
The sudden changes in scarid coloration generate ample confusion about their classification. It is believed, however, that the Indian Ocean alone hosts at least fifty different species of this family, all characterized by a blunt, rounded muzzle, a fused dentition, and big, flinty scales. Parrotfish are often consumed for food even though their meat is flabby and especially strong-flavored.

SCALPELS AND BRUSHES
The other principal herbivores on the reef are the so-called surgeonfish of the acanthurid family. Their common name derives from sharp horizontal blades on the caudal peduncle, which some species can pivot and turn forward at will. In at least one species, these dangerous scalpels are also connected to a poisonous gland.

Masked rabbitfish
Siganus puellus

228

Range Tropical western Pacific, Indian Ocean
Habitat Coastal waters and well developed reefs, 3–35 m (10–115 ft)
Size Up to 30 cm (12 in)
Description The young gather in small groups often mixed with specimens of other herbivorous species to graze among reef corals where they feed principally on the green algae that grow at the base of dead stony corals. Adults are almost always in pairs.

Stellate rabbitfish
Siganus stellatus

229

Range Indian Ocean as far as Java, Red Sea
Habitat Coastal reefs rich in invertebrates, 3–45 m (10–150 ft)
Size Up to 40 cm (16 in)
Description Like the preceding species, this one also has poisonous spines on its pectoral fins, capable of delivering painful wounds to potential aggressors. Adults form stable couples. Some consider the Red Sea population a species unto itself; it is easily recognized by a completely yellow tail.

Bluespine unicornfish
Naso unicornis

Range Tropical Indo-Pacific
Habitat Coastal reefs and slopes, 2–80 m (7–260 ft)
Size Up to 70 cm (27 in)
Description Immediately identifiable because of its large size, its gray-olive coloration, and the short, pointed protuberance on its forehead. Adults are often found in large shoals in the water column near slopes where they feed on plankton. Juveniles are herbivorous and stay in bays and lagoons less exposed to predators.

Bignose unicornfish
Naso vlamingii

Range Indian Ocean, tropical Indo-Pacific
Habitat Seaward reefs, slopes, channels in current, 2–50 m (7–165 ft)
Size Up to 55 cm (22 in)
Description Often forms loose shoals, seems to favor clear and deep waters including currents, yet also seeks out shallow seabeds where it passes the night inside cavities among the corals. Male adults assume a spectacular coloration during the mating season, when they do not even hesitate to approach divers up close.

Blacktongue unicornfish
Naso hexacanthus

Range Tropical Indo-Pacific
Habitat Seaward reefs and deep slopes, 10–50 m (33–165 ft) and beyond
Size Up to 70 cm (27 in)
Description A large and striking species, often in big shoals suspended in the water column near slopes where it feeds on plankton. Adult males can shift from the yellow-brown of their customary skin color to a soft blue within seconds. Like all surgeonfish, it has a large bladelike spine on both sides of its tail stem; these serve as defensive weapons.

180

Spotted unicornfish
Naso brevirostris

233

Range Tropical Indo-Pacific
Habitat Seaward reef and open waters, 2–80 m (7–260 ft)
Size Up to 50 cm (20 cm)
Description Easily recognized by its long prefrontal "horn" and finely speckled gray-green skin. In this species, too, adults prefer the water column in front of the reef while the young prefer reef shallows where they feed on algae.

Blue-spotted bristletooth
Ctenochaetus marginatus

234

Range Eastern Pacific Ocean
Habitat Coastal reefs and rocky outcroppings, 1–20 m (3–65 ft)
Size Up to 30 cm (12 in)
Description The habits of this surgeonfish are not well known, but like many of its cousins, it seems to represent a fundamental link in the chain of ciguatera poisoning. It feeds, in fact, on algae and diatoms, and their toxic properties are then deposited in its tissues and further transmitted to its predators in the food chain.

181

Yellowtail surgeonfish
Prionurus punctatus

235

Range Eastern tropical Indo-Pacific
Habitat Coastal reefs and rocky beds, 1–30 m (3–100 ft)
Size Up to 60 cm (23 in)
Description Often gathered in multitudinous shoals that graze along shallow rocky seabeds, where the undertow is strongest. It feeds mostly on algae. This is yet another species with strong scythelike spines at the base of its tail; these turn forward when the fish flexes its body and are used in intra-species duels and for defense.

Powderblue surgeonfish
Acanthurus leucosternon

236

Range Indian Ocean
Habitat Coastal waters, often in the undertow, 1–30 m (3–100 ft)
Size Up to 23 cm (9 in)
Description Habitually in small shoals, which can turn into immense aggregations near oceanic reefs, it seems to prefer shallow waters where wave action is felt the most. It feeds predominantly on algae, which it scrapes off corals using the surgeonfish's typical bristly teeth.

Blue tang
Acanthurus coeruleus

237

Range Atlantic Ocean, from New York to Brazil
Habitat Shallow reefs, 3–20 m (10–65 ft)
Size Up to 30 cm (12 in)
Description Sometimes solitary but more often in large shoals; sometimes in the company of other surgeonfish species. It feeds primarily on algae. The young are a brilliant yellow color; the change to the adults' powder blue or intense blue color begins as soon as fins appear.

Whitecheek surgeonfish

Acanthurus nigricans

238

Range Tropical Pacific Ocean

Habitat Reefs and rocky areas with undertow, 1–50 m (3–165 ft)

Size Up to 20 cm (8 in)

Description This species and the kindred *Acanthurus glaucopareius* are most easily observed when their small shoals whirl in the shallows among rocks and coral formations where wave action is the strongest. It feeds mostly on algae, which it scours from the substrate with its bristly teeth.

Sailfin tang

Zebrasoma veliferum

239

Range Tropical western Pacific Ocean

Habitat Coastal reefs, 2–30 m (7–100 ft)

Size Up to 40 cm (16 in)

Description Solitary in habit and only rarely found in pairs or groups, it is easily identified by its spectacular and delicately ornate coloration and its large dorsal and ventral fins, which it extends, however, only if menaced. Juveniles prefer lagoons rich with algae.

Heavybeak parrotfish
Chlorurus gibbus

Range Endemic to the Red Sea

Habitat Seaward and coastal reefs, 1–50 m (3–165 ft)

Size Up to 70 cm (27 in)

Description One of the most active coral "grazers" on the reef, usually gathered in small groups. The adult male is largely violet-green while the female tends to yellow-orange on the back and green on the belly and near the tail. Easily approached up close during the night, which it spends like all parrotfish wrapped in a cocoon of transparent mucus and hidden in a hollow among the corals.

Bullethead parrotfish
Chlorurus sordidus

Range Red Sea, tropical Indo-Pacific
Habitat Coral seabeds and lagoons, 1–25 m (3–80 ft)
Size Up to 40 cm (16 in)
Description Immature members and females are gregarious. This species can handle long excursions between its grazing grounds and nocturnal shelters. Many consider it the most common parrotfish in the Red Sea.

Bicolor parrotfish
Cetoscarus bicolor

Range Tropical Indo-Pacific
Habitat Seaward reefs and coral gardens, 1–40 m (3–130 ft)
Size Up to 90 cm (35 in)
Description Territorial and trailing a harem of females, adult males are characterized by a truly spectacular coloration, but they are very cautious and difficult to approach. The young are less than a few centimeters long with a totally different coloration (see inset photo), and are often common among the labyrinths of the reef.

Bridled parrotfish
Scarus frenatus

243

Range Tropical Indo-Pacific
Habitat Seaward reefs and coral drop-offs, 1–30 m (3–100 ft)
Size Up to 50 cm (20 in)
Description One of the most common Indo-Pacific parrotfish. The male is predominantly blue-green with pink lines, while the female tends to be brownish-red. It is often fished and consumed locally even though its flesh is flabby and has a rather disagreeable taste (a trait common to all algae-feeding fish).

Indian Ocean longnose parrotfish *Hipposcarus harid*

244

Range Red Sea, Indian Ocean
Habitat Lagoons and sandy reefs, 1–25 m (3–80 ft)
Size Up to 75 cm (29 in)
Description Sometimes observed in shoals with hundreds of specimens frenetically occupied with pulverizing the coral that they feed on with their robust teeth. At night, it can be approached effortlessly and immediately recognized by the pinkish color with blue streaks on its long muzzle and by lips that completely cover its beak.

187

Range Tropical Indo-Pacific
Habitat Well-developed coastal reefs, 3–40 m (10–130 ft)
Size Up to 55 cm (22 in)
Description Adult members habitually move in pairs, often mixed with other parrotfish or surgeonfish. Identification of this species is complicated by the chromatic variations of its coat, which changes radically according to the subject's age and sex and even the time of day or night when the individual is observed.

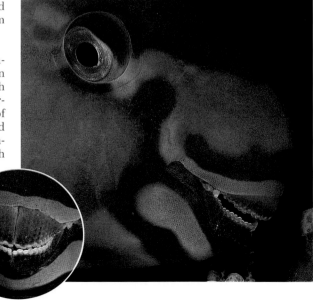

Dusky parrotfish
Scarus niger

Range Tropical Indo-Pacific
Habitat Coastal reefs and lagoons, 3–40 m (10–130 ft)
Size Up to 35 cm (14 in)
Description A species that seems to prefer sandy and detritus-strewn lagoon floors over all others. Easily identified by its purplish coloration and bright orange eye during the night, when it can be approached up close while it rests in its typical cocoon of transparent mucus.

Rusty parrotfish
Scarus ferrugineus

Range Red Sea, western Indian Ocean
Habitat Well-developed coastal reefs, 1–60 m (3–200 ft)
Size Up to 40 cm (16 in)
Description Adult males of this species form a harem of several females, generally between two and ten. Prefers more protected coral reefs and drop-offs rich in hiding places where it spends the night. It sleeps wedged among corals, wrapped in a cocoon of transparent mucus, like other members of the species.

Bumphead parrotfish
Bolbometopon muricatum

189

Range Tropical Indo-Pacific
Habitat Seaward reefs and deep slopes, 1–40 m (3–130 ft)
Size Up to 1.2 m (4 ft)
Description A large species with an exceptionally impressive appearance, it is characterized by big, hard, shell-like scales, a uniform green coloration, and the large, pink-tinged bulge on its forehead, which it sometimes uses as a battering ram to splinter corals. Adults travel great distances to reach their customary pastures, often crossing wide tracts of open ocean and always sleeping in the same burrows, usually large caves or wall fissures. During the day, they gather in "herds" of ten to thirty individuals and scour the reef at shallow depths, violently and noisily cropping corals with their powerful beaks, a behavior that reminds one of large, wild bovines feeding and justifiably earns them the nickname "bison fish."

SEA URCHINS

Sea urchins look more or less spherical, but the five segments of their calcareous skeleton clearly exhibit the characteristic structure of echinoderms. They are nocturnal animals, very common at shallow depths, sometimes not immediately visible. Once in the open, in fact, they are easily attacked by their enemies, so they prefer to spend daylight hours in the shelter of hollows from which it is impossible to extract them. Their chief enemies are the triggerfish that up-end them by gripping their long spines and then start eating them from the undefended ventral side. They feed on both plant and animal material and move around using the traction provided by their ambulacral pedicels—sophisticated water-vascular organs with rough terminals. The sexes are separate and reproduction occurs through the simultaneous release of eggs and sperm into the sea, followed by the development of pelagic larvae. Some species, such as the *Diadema setosum* and *D. antillarum*, are characterized by very long, thin quills that break on impact and cause painful infections at the affected site. Others such as the fire urchin, *Asthenosoma varium*, and the feared *Toxopneustes pileolus* can inflict extremely painful wounds that can even lead to death by cardiac arrest. Other species, such as the pencil urchins of

the genus *Heterocentrotus,* have inoffensive and rounded-off quills that limit them to mounting a purely mechanical obstacle in the face of predators. Small commensals are often observed among the spines of various urchins; these include the *Diademichthys lineatus* fish (see page 233) and the *Stegopontonia commensalis* shrimp.

1. *Asthenosoma varium*
Range Red Sea, central Indo-Pacific

2. *Mespilia globulus*
Range Central Indo-Pacific

3. *Tripneustes gratilla*
Range Red Sea, tropical Indo-Pacific

4. *Toxopneustes pileolus*
Range Tropical Indo-Pacific

5. *Heterocentrotus mammillatus*
Range Red Sea, central Indo-Pacific

6. *Phyllacanthus imperialis*
Range Tropical Indo-Pacific

7. *Diadema* sp.
Range Circumtropical

8. *Stegopontonia commensalis*
Range Tropical Indo-Pacific

GROUP STRATEGIES

Preceding pages: Yellowsaddle Goatfish, Red Sea

Predators and prey confront each other despite the ever-present risk of attack, trusting in the group strategy. A "squadron" of jacks has just attacked a formation of silversides (at right) by speeding across the school of small fish to take the slowest or oldest individuals unawares. Some species are social only when young, while others stay that way for their entire lives.

UNITED FOR SURVIVAL

Reef gazers often come across species preferring large groups that sometimes result in spectacular shoals composed of thousands of fish. This "group strategy" improves each individual's odds of survival in the highly competitive environment of the coral reef. Weak or small species adopt it, but so do big and clearly efficient predators. It is not by chance that more than half of marine fish species live in schools as juveniles and at least a quarter of the total continue to do so as adults. Pelagic hunters that lodge along the seaward slopes of the reef—especially dolphins, jacks and trevallys, tunas and barracudas, but also (off and on) certain species of shark—regularly adopt

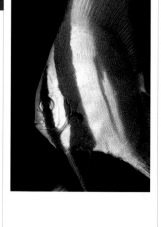

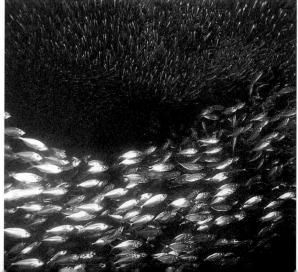

schooling strategies to hunt their prey. After methodically surrounding a victim, they attack with coordination and precision. Still, it is anything but simple for a large predator to select and focus its attack on a single prey in the face of a "living wall" made up of thousands of individuals that are perfectly coordinated in their movements. The wall will split open like an elusive and iridescent curtain only to snap closed again at the predators' backs. In such situations, the predator will focus on the weakest and slowest individuals who are quickly isolated from the rest of the shoal and eliminated. Some species commonly join big, largely temporary groups for courtship, reproduction and migration. The immense shoals of barracuda and sea bream found during the mating season near the Ras Muhammad promontory in Egypt are known worldwide. The reasons for large groupings of scalloped hammerhead sharks, *Sphyrna lewini,* near various oceanic peaks (Isla del Coco, Costa Rica; Sipadan and Layang Layang, Malaysia; and Malpelo, Colombia) are less clear even though they seem to be tied to a distinct social structure of that species.

Batfish of the genus Platax are typically social as juveniles and as adults. The young favor the shelter offered by jetties and piers.

Confounding the Enemy *Vital defensive and offensive operations are carried out by perfectly coordinating movements that convert the school into a gigantic meta-individual and by exploiting the predators' and victims' typically metallic and brilliant coloration, which facilitates the individuals' coordinated action while simultaneously confusing the opposing camp with gleaming reflections.*

THE SPECTACLE OF THE SHOALS

Few productions anywhere in the world deliver the same dramatic impact as a huge assembly of fish. These days, the ocean is the last place where humans can admire such impressive concentrations of individuals belonging to a sin-gle species. Fish gather in shoals for different reasons—to hunt, to escape their predators, to reproduce, or to migrate. The results are always spectacular, but nowadays often dangerous for the fish. With the advent of ultrasonic sounding gear, commercial fisheries can now cap-

ture thousands of individuals in a single stroke.

ALTOGETHER WITH FEELING

Surely one of the most surprising aspects of large shoals is the extraordinary synchrony of separate beings coordinating their movements and generating as a result a kind of single "individual" of gigantic proportions. Recent research indicates the important role of the "lateral line" in this behavior. This line of pores falls horizontally along the fishes' flanks and is used by individuals to register microvariations of pressure in their surroundings.

POLARIZED LIGHT

Species that spend the better part of their existence in shoals have metallic colorations with distinctive iridescent reflections (like the typical "bluefish" of the Mediterranean). Observed underwater, this coloration will polarize depending upon the fish's position in relation to the incidence of ambient light. In a split second, the school's silvery curtain becomes a confused and blurry fog. Thus, a shoal of fish laid bare to invasion by one or more predators deploys fast, slanting actions and furiously changes course to confound the attack.

CURTAIN CALLS

Another strategy involves keeping the formation tight while opening a space around the attacker, only to reunite instantly on the other side. To capture its quarry, the predator must focus on the slowest individuals, which usually gravitate to the edges of the school, or it must succeed in slamming into the shoal at lightning speed and stunning its members with the mere force of the strike.

Boer's spadefish
Platax boersii

Range Central Indo-Pacific
Habitat Seaward reefs and slopes, 0.5–50 m (1.5–165 ft)
Size Up to 40 cm (16 in)
Description Often in dense aggregations on pelagic reefs and near deep-water slopes; sometimes confused with its cousin *P. orbicularis* from which it can be distinguished by the different profile of its snout. The species was only recently identified. Like all batfish, it feeds on algae, jellyfish and small benthic organisms.

Dusky batfish
Platax pinnatus

Range Western Pacific Ocean
Habitat Seaward reefs and slopes, 2–50 m (7–165 ft)
Size Up to 35 cm (14 in)
Description Adults, which can be identified by a fairly pointed snout, often gather in great shoals. The young—immediately identifiable by their characteristic brown or black color trimmed in vivid orange (see photo)—are solitary and found under jetties or in caves.

Longfin batfish
Platax teira

Range Red Sea, tropical Indo-Pacific
Habitat Coastal and seaward reefs, 0.5–60 m (1.5–200 ft)
Size Up to 60 cm (23 in)
Description Common and approachable, they generally gather in multitudinous shoals. Recognized by the elaboration of the dorsal and ventral fins and by its coloration—lightly banded in brownish-black on silver. The young have a marked vertical development and often hover in small groups in the shelter of jetties or floating debris.

 199

Orbicular batfish
Platax orbicularis

Range Red Sea, tropical Indo-Pacific
Habitat Seaward reefs, 0.5–40 m (1.5–130 ft)
Size Up to 50 cm (20 in)
Description A *Platax* with a distinctively discoid profile, often swimming in huge shoals near reef slopes. The young are brownish-orange in color and look much like dead leaves. They position themselves in the extreme shallows of sandy and muddy seabeds, half perched on one flank and skillfully mimicking the vegetable debris lying on the bottom.

GROUP STRATEGIES

Sardines, herrings, anchovies
Aterinidi, Clupeidi, Engraulidi

Range Circumtropical
Habitat Shallow pelagic waters, 1–20 m (3–65 ft)
Size Up to 12 cm (4.5 in)
Description Several families and many species are nearly identical in appearance and hard to differentiate underwater. In general, they form dense shoals of hundreds or thousands of individuals whose movements are perfectly synchronized. Their typically polarized, silvery coloration confuses and distracts predators. Found in open waters and often inside caves, crevices and wrecks.

Striped eel catfish
Plotosus lineatus

254

Range Tropical Indo-Pacific
Habitat Muddy and sandy seabeds, areas of detritus, 1–50 m (3–165 ft)
Size up to 35 cm (14 in)
Description The only catfish found in coral reefs, they can inflict very painful wounds with spines on their fins connected to poisonous glands with a highly toxic, but rarely lethal, secretion. They move frenetically along the seabed in almost spherical groups and operate like steamrollers, rummaging continually on the bottom for small invertebrates.

Yellowsaddle goatfish
Parupeneus cyclostomus

255

Range Red Sea, tropical Indo-Pacific
Habitat Coral and mixed seabeds, 3–100 m (10–330 ft)
Size Up to 40 cm (16 in)
Description A large species with variable colorations but often bright yellow in adults. It hunts actively during the day by vigorously foraging in the substrate with its characteristic barbels. In its search for food, it is often accompanied by labrids of the genus *Thalassoma,* which profit from its activity. Habitually in large groups, only rarely alone.

Yellowfin goatfish
Mulloidichthys vanicolensis

256

Range Red Sea, tropical Indo-Pacific
Habitat Mixed seabeds, 5–100 m (16–330 ft)
Size Up to 35 cm (14 in)
Description This mullet often assembles into large shoals. Relatively inactive during the day, it moves along sandbanks at night and rummages in the substrate to find the little invertebrates it eats.

Sawtooth barracuda
Sphyraena putnamiae

Range Red Sea, tropical Indo-Pacific
Habitat Seaward reefs and open waters, 10–100 m (30–330 ft)
Size Up to 1 m (3 ft)
Description Generally gather in extremely dense, fairly sedentary schools shaped like a vortex and containing hundreds of individuals. These living "tornadoes" can often be observed near deep-water slopes or in the vicinity of pelagic reefs. Single individuals separate from the school only to hunt at dawn or sundown. Easy to confuse underwater with the species on the opposite page; the blackish coloration of the tail fin is diagnostic, as are numerous darker bands on the body, which has the typical metallic shine.

Pickhandle barracuda
Sphyraena jello

258

Range Tropical Indo-Pacific
Habitat Seaward reefs and slopes, 1–100 m (3–330 ft)
Size Up to 1.5 m (5 ft)
Description A large species normally gathered in dense schools during the day, especially when young. Hard to distinguish underwater from similar species; in theory, the darker lateral-dorsal line broken in mid-flank and yellowish tail fin are diagnostic in adults. This species seems to prefer deep waters.

Blackfin barracuda
Sphyraena qenie

259

Range Red Sea, tropical Indo-Pacific
Habitat Deep seabeds and slopes, 10–50 m (33–165 ft)
Size Up to 1.5 m (5 ft)
Description This large species is usually grouped in dense shoals during the day. Rather hard to distinguish from others in its genus if sighted underwater; theoretically identified by its longitudinal blue dorsal line, which is difficult to discern underwater.

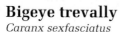

Bigeye trevally
Caranx sexfasciatus

260

Range Red Sea, tropical Indo-Pacific

Habitat Seaward reefs and slopes, 3–100 m (10–330 ft)

Size Up to 85 cm (33 in)

Description The most social carangid (see page 38 for other species in this family of pelagic predators). Usually gathered in spectacular, fairly sedentary vortex shoals with hundreds of members. The young prefer coastal waters and the protected environment of estuaries, while adults are more easily observed near deep sea floors. Immense aggregations of adults have some-times been observed in Malaysian waters as they fell prey to the *Gymnosarda unicolor* tunas and various shark species.

Males assume a very dark coloration during the mating season and separate temporarily from the school to isolate the most receptive females.

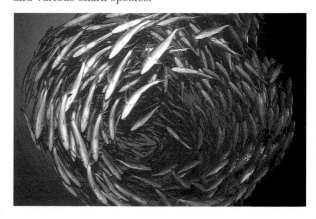

Bluestreak fusilier
Pterocaesio tile

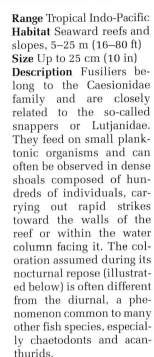

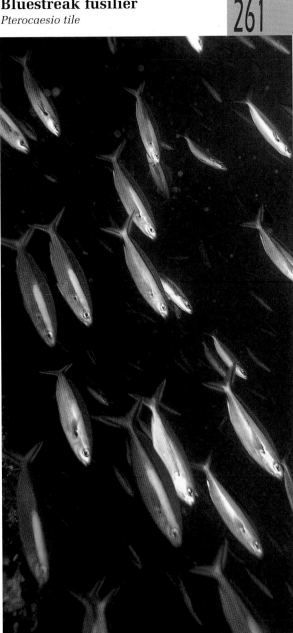

Range Tropical Indo-Pacific
Habitat Seaward reefs and slopes, 5–25 m (16–80 ft)
Size Up to 25 cm (10 in)
Description Fusiliers belong to the Caesionidae family and are closely related to the so-called snappers or Lutjanidae. They feed on small planktonic organisms and can often be observed in dense shoals composed of hundreds of individuals, carrying out rapid strikes toward the walls of the reef or within the water column facing it. The coloration assumed during its nocturnal repose (illustrated below) is often different from the diurnal, a phenomenon common to many other fish species, especially chaetodonts and acanthurids.

Randall's fusilier
Pterocaesio randalli

262

Range Central Indo-Pacific
Habitat Seaward reefs and slopes, 6–35 m (20–115 ft)
Size Up to 22 cm (8.5 in)
Description Recognized by the bright yellow blotch that adorns its flanks. It forms large, dense shoals composed of hundreds of individuals and, like all fusiliers, is a superb and fast swimmer.

Lunar fusilier
Caesio lunaris

263

Range Red Sea, tropical Indo-Pacific
Habitat Slopes and seaward reefs, 2–40 m (7–130 ft)
Size Up to 25 cm (10 in)
Description A very common species along the slopes and walls of seaward reefs, usually assembled in dense shoals containing hundreds of individuals. Like all fusiliers, the shoals can launch sudden and spectacular movements toward divers only to distance themselves as rapidly and in unison.

Yellowback fusilier
Caesio teres

Range Tropical Indo-Pacific
Habitat Seaward reefs, 1–40 m (3–130 ft)
Size Up to 26 cm (10 in)
Description A very common species in the Indian Ocean, it usually congregates in great shoals that stay in continuous motion in the water column opposite the reef. Feeds on zooplankton like all of its cousins.

Deep-bodied fusilier
Caesio cuning

Range Central tropical Indo-Pacific
Habitat Coastal and seaward reefs, 3–40 m (10 - 130 ft)
Size Up to 40 cm (16 in)
Description The biggest fusilier, and oldest living member of the species; represented by numerous regional subspecies that are more or less similar. Sometimes it is embellished with yellow in the tail area. Often collected in dense shoals hunting zooplankton in the water column opposite the reef.

Five-lined snapper
Lutjanus quinquelineatus

Range Tropical Indo-Pacific
Habitat Various environments, 2–40 m (7–130 ft)
Size Up to 38 cm (15 in)
Description This snapper (see also pages 70 to 73) often gathers in immense sedentary shoals with hundreds of others that separate to hunt alone once darkness falls. Common in shallows, lagoons and off embankments, often in the shelter of large hollows or jutting ledges.

208

Bluelined snapper
Lutjanus kasmira

Range Tropical Indo-Pacific
Habitat Various environments, 5–250 m (16–820 ft)
Size Up to 35 cm (14 in)
Description A very common species in various environments from lagoons to steep banks, often gathered in dense sedentary shoals containing hundreds of individuals. At night the shoals disperse and single individuals hunt separately. Its white belly and four (rather than five) longitudinal blue stripes distinguish this species at first glance from the five-lined snapper.

Yellowspot emperor
Gnathodentex aurolineatus

Range Tropical Indo-Pacific
Habitat Lagoons and protected reefs, 5–30 m (16–100 ft)
Size Up to 30 cm (12 in)
Description Unlike other emperorfish, this member of the Lethrinidae family has distinctly social habits, sometimes gathering in shoals of hundreds of individuals. It favors tranquil waters and is capable of suddenly changing the tonalities of its plain attire but always keeping the distinctive yellow patch on its back.

Sweepers
Parapriacanthus sp.

Range Red Sea, tropical Indo-Pacific
Habitat Reefs and coral drop-offs, 10–50 m (30–165 ft)
Size Up to 10 cm (4 in)
Description They gather in compact shoals of hundreds, and are found in cavities, caves and often shipwrecks. They look like an undulating, permeable, golden, iridescent curtain. At night, they disperse and hunt individually for zooplankton. *Parapriacanthus* and *Pempheris* genera are represented by various similar species.

MIMICRY

MASTERS OF DECEIT

At first glance, the world of the coral reef may look like a kingdom of gaudy costumes and flamboyant colors. In reality, however, many of its inhabitants deftly employ sophisticated mimetic techniques to render themselves as inconspicuous as possible, both to procure food and to avoid becoming food for predators. These objectives are frequently coupled to one another. Even the large pelagic species that frequent the seaward walls of the reef adopt this regimen. Sharks and manta rays are just two that embrace the technique called counter-

The reef inhabitants' mimetic and camouflage skills are a continuing source of marvel for divers. Above, one of the authors observes a small frog-fish up close as it sits in ambush on its usual perch—in this case, a matching sponge. At right, dynamic polychromes act to conceal the body of this scorpionfish.

Preceding page: Shortfin Lionfish, Indian Ocean

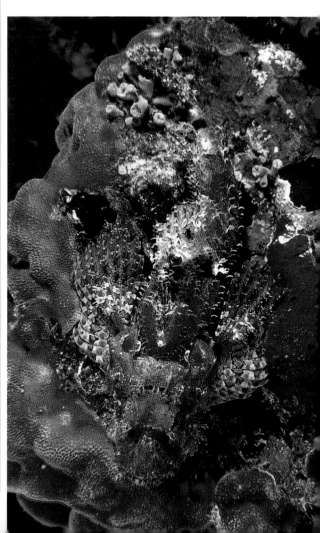

shading, which inspired humans to achieve air superiority by camouflaging military aircraft. Viewed from above, the animal's dark gray or bluish back blends with the shadowy depths beneath, while its pale or white belly makes it nearly invisible against the backdrop of the surface when the animal is seen from below, against the light of the sun's rays. There are great pelagic predators that hunt instead in the shallow layers of open water and have adopted a typically "chromium-plated" and glossy coloration, interrupted at intervals by more or less dark vertical bands. They rely on sudden bursts and speed, and this coloration helps them blend effectively into the mottled shadows of shallows where the sun's penetration and wave action are more intense. With the exception of tunas, barracuda and carangids, these species are mostly outside the scope of this book. For additional advantages offered by the metallic coloration adopted most often by these formidable predators, we

Octopuses (above), cuttlefish and squid—represented in tropical waters by various genera and species—are probably the most refined makeup and sleight-of-hand artists. Avidly hunted by bottom-fishing groupers, moray eels and sharks, the coral reef's cephalopods are subject to a more intense predation than are those in temperate seas. To survive such a hostile place, they must take recourse to all the skills refined during their evolutionary history.

The Role of Chromatophores

Chromatophores are highly specialized skin cells that determine an animal's color (as though they were full of pixels). In some cases, they can be dilated or contracted at will, allowing the animal to modify its coloration by "regulating" the intensity of its colors. Many reptiles and amphibians have refined this ability on dry land. Underwater, cephalopod mollusks such as octopuses and cuttlefish can modify their superficial skin tissue instantaneously (photo at bottom right) and thus change their pigmentation immediately. Here it could be said that the art of mimicry is converted into philosophy. The ichthyic species' shift from an admittedly sophisticated passivity to a dynamic application of their biological functions ultimately crosses the frontier into abstract reasoning.

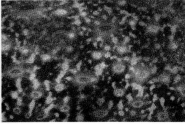

Who could imagine that this clump of dead coral encrusted with calcareous algae is really a scorpionfish lying in ambush? The predator's immobility—sustained to the last instant—will contribute to maintaining the illusion.

refer the reader to the chapter dedicated to "group strategies" (page 192). The big pelagic hunters generally exploit counter-shaded but substantially uniform colorations because the undifferentiated backdrop of open waters would not offer advantages to spotted or striped patterns, rendering the animal easier to spot. On the other hand, there are stripings and specklings that prove far more advantageous to species with more rooted habits. A "somatolitic" species is capable of altering its shape by obscuring its contours against an equally kaleidoscopic backdrop (like those adopted by certain terrestrial snakes, for example). Among families that distinguish themselves in the application of this formula, the true standouts are cobrafish and scorpionfish (Scorpaenidae), pipefish (Syngnathidae) and frogfish (Antennariidae). These creatures often combine the advantages offered by striped and mottled flesh to those provided by inflatable skin appendages and by a body that—in the most extreme cases—looks like anything but a fish. Many are illustrated in the following pages. The effectiveness of mimicry is optimized in several species by habits, posture and by the animal's bodily structure. The *Synanceia verrucosa* stonefish maintains such a scrupulous immobility that it is often covered with algae and hydroids that contribute to its camouflage; the ghost pipefish, *Solenos-*

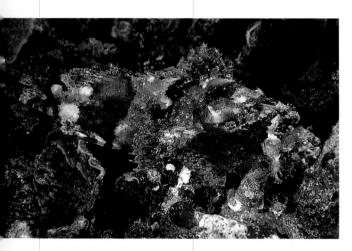

The Advantages of Disruptive Coloration

The gaudy colors of certain species can prove unusually mimetic. The windowpane scheme (similar to a tartan) that earmarks the little longnose hawkfish, Oxycirrhithes typus, *is perfectly functional in the densely laced environment of gorgonian and black coral colonies where this small predator lives. In deep waters, the vivid white-and-carmine*

checkerboard illuminated by the artificial light of the flash in this photograph will play a practical function by discreetly "breaking up" the animal's shape.

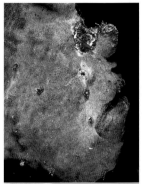

Predators that hunt by lying in ambush—like the devil scorpionfish at left—are often poor swimmers and they cannot afford to make mistakes on the first attack. For this reason, they usually have an extremely large mouth whose lightning-fast opening (below, a frogfish) generates a violent suction that usually prevents the prey's escape.

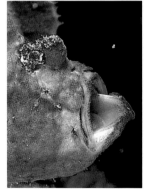

tomus spp., stand in a head-down, vertical position; and turbot and sole are distinctively flattened, and frogfish have evolved pawlike pectoral fins to better grip sponges. If mimetic techniques and camouflage are largely typical of species that use appearances to hunt, there are many occasions when a species uses the so-called Batesian mimicry—a theory named after H.W. Bates, one of the first scientists to study it (1862)— to pass itself off for another. The little blenny predator *Aspidontus taeniatus* gets close to its victims by making itself look like the worthy common cleaner wrasse, *Labroides dimidiatus*; and the larval stage of the sea cucumber, *Bohadschia graffei*, assumes a color and shape nearly identical to the inedible and poisonous sea slug *Phyllidia varicosa*. Examples of this mimicry are numerous and intriguing. It will also be useful to remember the effective and surprising function carried out by the chromatophores or specialized skin cells in many species. They ultimately determine the animal's coloration and may sometimes be dilated or contracted at will, allowing the animal to change its own color.

THE ART OF DECEPTION

The phenomena involved in mimicry are among the most fascinating on the coral reef. There is no apparent end to the ingenuity of solutions adopted by predators and prey to trick each other. Some species pass themselves off as others while others prefer to masquerade as part of their setting.

EYES AND TENDONS

When a predator like Beaufort's crocodilefish lies half-buried in the sand bottom, the only element that could possibly attract the attention of

another predator or alarm a potential victim is its big protruding eye. Contributing to its disguise—as well as reducing the intensity of ambient light—the crocodilefish (and several other species, such as the spotted ray) have evolved a filamentous and radial "eyelid" that hides the animal's eye to perfection.

THE KEY IS TO CONFUSE
To our eyes, and once illuminated artificially by a flash, many scorpaenids seem more gaudy than mimetic. In reality, their bright coloration in red and brown tones, the irregular contour of their "ornamentation," and the large number of their appendages, tendrils and warts succeed in making them disappear on a seabed of coral formations that swarms with life and color. Some land snakes—such as the dangerous Bitis gabonica viper found in Gabon—seem exceedingly flashy if observed on a neutral ground but can disappear before the viewer's eyes when resting motionless on a bed of rotting leaves or in shadow. In any case, these animals find themselves completely defenseless if forced away from their habitat.

SHALL WE EXAGGERATE?
The phenomena involved in camouflage approach the extreme in some species. The dangerous Synanceia verrucosa stonefish lies stock-still for so long that it ends up covered with algae and hydroids, which contribute to making it invisible. The decoy scorpionfish, Iracundus signifer, has turned its own dorsal fin into a copy of a tiny fish perched on the seabed. Predators that approach to swallow what looks like an easy victim, perched immobile on a stone covered with algae, end up being deceived and devoured. The big, robust ghost pipefish, Solenostomus cyanopterus—similar to a broken frond of seagrass—even exhibits colored blotches that simulate an encrustation of calcareous algae that distinguishes the plant it imitates.

Peacock flounder
Bothus mancus

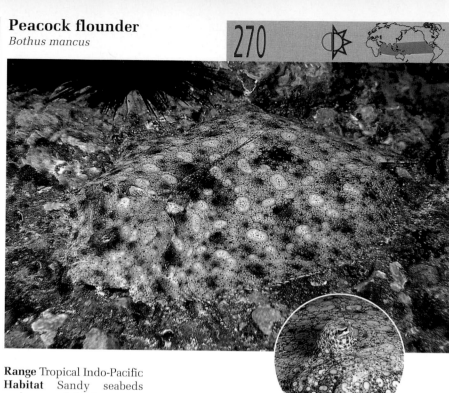

Range Tropical Indo-Pacific
Habitat Sandy seabeds and areas of detritus, 1–85 m (3–280 ft)
Size Up to 45 cm (18 in)
Description This large species has a seemingly gaudy coloration that provides superb camouflage in practice. In the tropical Indo-Pacific alone, there are more than fifteen genera and ninety different species in the Bothidae or lefteye flounder family, all more or less resembling one another but always characterized by both eyes being on the left side of an unusually compressed body. They feed on fish and small benthic organisms.

Banded sole
Soleichthys heterohinos

271

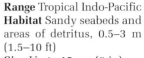

Range Tropical Indo-Pacific
Habitat Sandy seabeds and areas of detritus, 0.5–3 m (1.5–10 ft)
Size Up to 15 cm (6 in)
Description A typical sole found on muddy or sandy seabeds in lagoons or reef beds that are less heavily pounded. Nocturnal, it swims near the substrate with an undulatory motion. During the day, it lies half-buried in sand on the bottom.

219

Peacock sole
Pardachirus pavoninus

272

Range Western Pacific and Indian Ocean
Habitat Sandy and muddy seabeds, 3–40 m (10–130 ft)
Size Up to 22 cm (8.5 in)
Description Characteristic of sandy or muddy seabeds, it is another of more than 100 species (in thirty genera) that make up the sole or Soleidae family. This benthic predator has a pectoral sac that can release a milky toxic liquid as a deterrent in case of danger; both eyes are characteristically located on the right side of their eminently compressed bodies.

Bartel's dragonet
Synchiropus bartelsi

273

Range From Indonesia to the Philippines
Habitat Areas of detritus, 3–35 m (10–115 ft)
Size Up to 4.5 cm (1.75 in)
Description Relatively common on rubbly bottoms in shallow water but extremely difficult to spot by virtue of its camouflage. It moves in rapid spurts and is loath to leave the bottom. This and the following species are similar to *S. splendidus* (see page 139) and *S. picturatus*, known as "psychedelic fish" for the flashiness of their coloration.

Ocellated dragonet
Synchiropus ocellatus

274

Range Tropical Indo-Pacific from Indonesia to Japan
Habitat Seabeds with detritus, 1–50 m (3–165 ft)
Size Up to 6.5 cm (2.5 in)
Description Common enough locally on bottoms with rubble and in tide pools, it is a sedentary species with territorial behavior. It moves in spurts without going far from the bottom.

Ornate pipefish
Halicampus macrorhynchus

Range Tropical Indo-Pacific
Habitat Sandy and muddy
seabeds, 1–25 m (3–80 ft)
Size Up to 20 cm (8 in)
Description This species is
characteristic of sandy and
muddy bottoms and has
exceptional mimetic skills,
acquiring algal growths at
shallow depths. Its back
and snout have numerous
skin flaps that shrink over
time.

Seagrass filefish
Acreichthys tomentosus

Range Central Indo-Pacific
Habitat Corroding reefs,
jetties, sandy drop-offs,
1–25 m (3–80 ft)
Size Up to 7 cm (2.75 in)
Description Sedentary, mas-
terfully camouflaged by
its skin protuber-
ances and fila-
ments, it can be
observed with
a certain fre-
quency near
the pylons that
hold up jetties,
the habitat of
choice for many
species with obvious
mimetic abilities.

Harlequin ghost pipefish
Solenostomus paradoxus

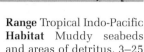

Range Tropical Indo-Pacific
Habitat Muddy seabeds and areas of detritus, 3–25 m (10–80 ft)

Size Up to 10 cm (4 in)
Description A relatively common species, sedentary, often found in pairs but most often overlooked by divers because of its extraordinary camouflage. Limited like its cousins to calm seabeds, it often perches near the substrate or among gorgonian branches and maintains its characteristic head-down, vertical posture. Its body is spotted with black, red, yellow and white. It feeds mostly on tiny crustaceans sucked in with its elongated snout.

Ghost pipefish
Solenostomus cyanopterus

Range Tropical Indo-Pacific
Habitat Seagrass flats and areas of detritus, 3–25 m (10–80 ft)
Size Up to 15 cm (6 in)
Description Relatively common locally but hard to spot, its lean body is covered with bony rings. A vertical, head-down stance is maintained right next to the bottom; and its coloration helps camouflage it to perfection among drifting seagrass fronds.

223

Thorny seahorse
Hippocampus hystrix

279

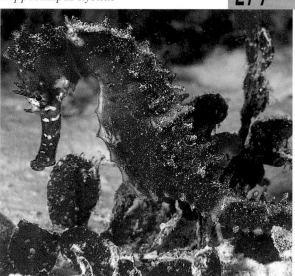

Range Tropical Indo-Pacific
Habitat Sandy bottoms with abundant vegetation, 1–20 m (3–65 ft)
Size Up to 15 cm (6 in)
Description Almost always in pairs, motionless near the bottom, it clasps onto vegetation using its prehensile tail. Males in the Syngnathidae family—seahorses and pipefish—tend the family eggs in a specially designed brood pouch until they hatch. Commercial fisheries serving the Chinese herbal drug market gravely threaten the species.

Commerson's frogfish
Antennarius commersonii

Range Tropical Indo-Pacific, Red Sea

Habitat Protected reefs, 1–50 m (3–165 ft)

Size Up to 30 cm (12 in)

Description The antennariid family includes twelve genera and more than forty-one different species found all over the world in tropical waters. Some species are less than a few centimeters long; others spread to football size; the one illustrated can be considered typical. Sedentary and territorial predators, the antennariids have a highly specialized predatory instrument. It is composed of the *illicium* (a thin, transparent frontal antenna) and the *esca* (a fragment of fleshy tissue on the tip of the *illicium* that mimics small prey such as worms and acts as a lure). The whole apparatus is moved at will in front of the fish's huge mouth, which flaps open suddenly to gulp down the prey when it approaches and succumbs to the tempting lure that is so artfully jiggled. Antennariids feed almost exclusively on other fish and are capable of devouring specimens as long as they are. Relatively common in the most protected parts of the reef, they are extremely difficult to spot because of their stubby, irregular profile and exceptionally well-camouflaged body. They are known as frogfish because their pectoral fins actually resemble palmate or limblike feet. Antennariids station themselves on carefully chosen perches and generally do not abandon them for several years. They prefer candelabra sponges whose color and surface design they duplicate to perfection.

Stonefish
Synanceia verrucosa

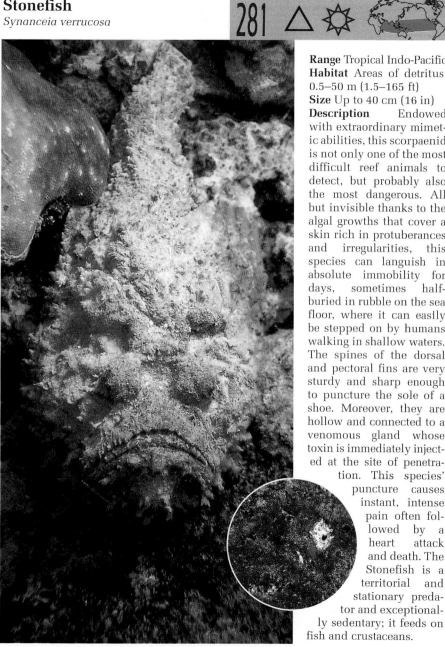

Range Tropical Indo-Pacific
Habitat Areas of detritus,
0.5–50 m (1.5–165 ft)
Size Up to 40 cm (16 in)
Description Endowed
with extraordinary mimet-
ic abilities, this scorpaenid
is not only one of the most
difficult reef animals to
detect, but probably also
the most dangerous. All
but invisible thanks to the
algal growths that cover a
skin rich in protuberances
and irregularities, this
species can languish in
absolute immobility for
days, sometimes half-
buried in rubble on the sea
floor, where it can easily
be stepped on by humans
walking in shallow waters.
The spines of the dorsal
and pectoral fins are very
sturdy and sharp enough
to puncture the sole of a
shoe. Moreover, they are
hollow and connected to a
venomous gland whose
toxin is immediately inject-
ed at the site of penetration. This species'
puncture causes
instant, intense
pain often fol-
lowed by a
heart attack
and death. The
Stonefish is a
territorial and
stationary preda-
tor and exceptional-
ly sedentary; it feeds on
fish and crustaceans.

Devil scorpionfish
Scorpaenopsis diabolus

282 △ ☼

Range Red Sea, tropical Indo-Pacific
Habitat Seaward reefs and lagoons, 1–70 m (3–230 ft)
Size Up to 20 cm (8 in)
Description Perfectly camouflaged among corals or rubble, if disturbed, it spreads its pectoral fins showing their warning coloration and alternating yellow, black and orange bands. It can deliver painful wounds with its poisonous dorsal spines.

Raggy scorpionfish
Scorpaenopsis venosa

283 △ ☼

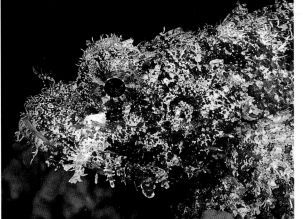

Range Tropical Indo-Pacific
Habitat Seabeds rich in sponges and soft corals, 3–55 m (10–180 ft)
Size Up to 25 cm (10 in)
Description A species difficult to distinguish from many other similar ones, it is characterized by its variable but clearly mimetic coloration and sedentary habits. It hunts by waiting and feeds primarily on fish and crustaceans. The spines on its dorsal fins are linked to a poisonous gland and their sting invariably proves very painful.

Flasher scorpionfish
Scorpaenopsis macrochir

284 △ ☼

Range Tropical Indo-Pacific
Habitat Areas of detritus, 1–30 m (3–100 ft)
Size Up to 12 cm (4.5 in)
Description A small scorpionfish characterized by its big eyes, the unmistakable "hump" behind its head, and by the vivid aposematic or cautionary coloring on its inner pectoral fins, which are displayed in a flash in case of threat. It rests motionless on the bottom and feeds chiefly on the small fish and crustaceans it ambushes.

Tassled scorpionfish
Scorpaenopsis oxycephalus

285 △ ☼

Range Red Sea, tropical Indo-Pacific
Habitat Seaward reefs and lagoons, 3–55 m (10–180 ft)
Size Up to 40 cm (16 in)
Description Characteristic of the reef and hard to differentiate from many others like it, all typified by a polychromatic body that is at once highly variable and obviously mimetic. Just about invisible when it lies motionless among corals, its vivid coloration is revealed in the light of a flash. Like all scorpaenids, its spines are venomous.

Shortfin lionfish
Dendrochirus brachypterus

Range Tropical Indo-Pacific
Habitat Areas of detritus and turbid waters, 1–100 m (3–330 ft)
Size Up to 15 cm (6 in)
Description Difficult to spot on its home ground because of its small size and formidably mimetic costume. Its coloration is extremely variable. Like many other scorpaenids, when threatened, it assumes a spectacular cautionary posture by spreading its wide pectoral fins with their multicolored and iridescent ocelli.

228

Spiny devilfish
Inimicus didactylus

287 △ ☼

Range Tropical Indo-Pacific
Habitat Muddy and sandy seabeds, 1–40 m (3–130 ft)
Size Up to 20 cm (8 in)
Description This species uses the first three unfettered spines on its pectoral fins to "walk" on the bottom. Recognized by the long poisonous spines on its dorsal fin and by its prognathous snout that juts out. Represented in the Red Sea by the *I. filamentosus* species.

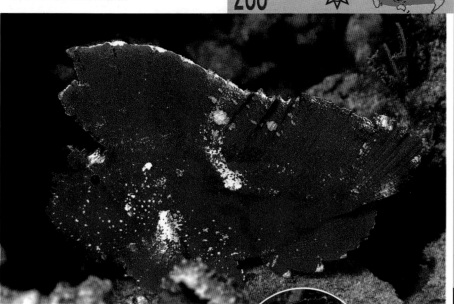

229

Range Tropical Indo-Pacific
Habitat Coastal and seaward reefs, 1–100 m (3–330 ft)
Size Up to 12 cm (4.5 in)
Description This very interesting species is characterized by a remarkably variable coloration (the most frequent ground colors are white, brown, bright red, green and yellow) that is superbly mimetic, a compressed body, and a habit of changing its skin all at once by sloughing off a transparent sheath much like snakes. Leaf scorpionfish are fairly common locally but always hard to detect. They are small, stationary and sedentary predators that sometimes stay near the same stretch of reef for years. Territorial in behavior, they are sometimes found in small loose groups in the same locality. If closely approached, they try to deceive the observer by pretending to be algae swaying in the current and by adopting a characteristic lateral wave motion, which they also use routinely to approach their prey. Leaf scorpionfish usually feed on small fish and crustaceans.

Pacific graysby
Epinephelus panamensis

289

Range Eastern Pacific from California to Peru
Habitat Rocky seabeds and crevices, 5–30 m (16–100 ft)
Size Up to 50 cm (20 in)
Description This grouper is superbly camouflaged by its olive or reddish colors spotted with white. It is easily approached while motionless, awaiting the approach of potential prey. It feeds on fish and crustaceans. (See page 98 for other species of grouper.)

Spotted sand-diver
Trichonotus setiger

290

Range Tropical Indo-Pacific
Habitat Sandy coastal seabeds, 3–40 m (10–130 ft)
Size Up to 25 cm (10 in)
Description Limited to sandy and loose seabeds, this species spends most of its time perched on the bottom or buried in the sand and occasionally showing part of its snout. If disturbed it darts under the sand and reappears again, sometimes one or two meters away.

Beaufort's crocodilefish
Cymbacephalus beauforti

Range Tropical Pacific Ocean as far as Japan

Habitat Rubbly seabeds on reefs and lagoons, 1–30 m (3 to 100 ft)

Size Up to 60 cm (23 in)

Description Closely related to the Indian Ocean crocodilefish, *Papilloculiceps longiceps*, this big, powerful predator is easily observed while it waits motionless and perfectly camouflaged for its prey on the summit of the reef or perched on rubble along the seabed. Innocuous despite its big thorny head, large mouth and formidable looks, it can suddenly change the chromatic intensity of its coat. Adults display a typically somatolitic coloration (see inset photo) whose labyrinthine flourishes (an outright brilliant blue in some individuals!) achieve the practical effect of "disintegrating" the fish's body against the mottled backdrop of the substrate. Juveniles are almost completely black and look like rotting branches lying static on the seabed. It feeds on fish and crustaceans that it catches by ambush.

Fringelip flathead
Eurycephalus otaitensis

Range Tropical Indo-Pacific
Habitat Sandy and rubbly seabeds, 1–30 m (3–100 ft)
Size Up to 25 cm (10 in)
Description Usually spends daylight hours half-buried in the substrate and sets out to hunt during the night. If illuminated artificially by a flash, it assumes delicate iridescent hues. Crocodilefish generally lack swim bladders, making any separation from the seabed difficult. They number more than sixty species divided among eighteen genera.

Cuttlefish
Sepia latimanus

293

Range Tropical Indo-Pacific
Habitat Sandy, muddy, and coralline seabeds, 5–20 m (16–65 ft)
Size Up to 60 cm (23 in)
Description Easily approached and animated by a certain speculative intelligence. Characterized by a mantle bristling with appendages and warts, it can change its outer pattern and color with stupefying speed. It feeds mostly on fish and crustaceans.

Octopus
Octopus sp.

Range Cosmopolitan
Habitat Rocky areas, reefs, lagoons, 1–20 m (3–65 ft)
Size Up to 1 m (3 ft)
Description Represented in every hot and temperate sea by numerous species that are different but are all objectively "intelligent." The most common Indo-Pacific species is *O. cyaneus*, while *O. vulgaris*, *macropus*, and *burryi* are common in the Caribbean. The venomous bite of the blue-ringed octopus, *Hapalochlaena lunulata*, is very dangerous; it is widespread in the central Pacific.

Urchin clingfish
Diademichthys lineatus

Range Tropical Indo-Pacific
Habitat Almost exclusively among the spines of *Diadema* sea urchins
Size Up to 5 cm (2 in)
Description A species observed almost exclusively among the long, sharp spines of sea urchins in the *Diadema* genus, an almost impenetrable defense against most predators. Alternatively, other species of the *Discotrema* genus in the same family live almost exclusively in association with crinoids (see page 166).

RELATIONSHIPS

MARRIAGES OF CONVENIENCE

Many of the reef's innumerable species have developed intriguing and close relationships based on mutual interest in a highly competitive universe. Generally known as symbiosis, this relationship is called *mutualism* if its advantages apply to both species involved and *commensalism* when only one partner benefits (it would be *parasitism* if the host is damaged). We are still a long way, though, from being able to draw precise distinctions in most of the known cases. Perhaps the best known of these curious and fascinating "marriages of convenience" is the one that transpires between various species of damselfish in the *Amphiprion* genus and large sea anemones. The young fish gradually develop total immunity to their hosts' poisonous nematocysts—whose stinging tentacles prove fatal for other fish—and they don't stray far from the microenvironment within the big anemone. Other visitors that also find anemones convenient are various species of crustaceans such as the numerous crabs in the *Periclemenes* genus (now and then also found on big nudibranchs, sea cucumbers, urchins and starfish) and the porcelain crab in the *Neopetrolisthes* genus. In this case, however, commensalism is the more accurate term inasmuch as no obvious advantages accrue to the host organism from the presence of the small crustaceans. On the other hand, a clearly mutualistic relationship unites the little alpheid shrimp with the characteristic gobies on muddy and sandy seabeds. These two species share a burrow—a tunnel dug into

The symbiotic relationship between parrotfish (above) or porcelain crabs (below) and their host anemones generates mutual advantages. Both are shielded from predators in separate ways.

Preceding page: Orange Anemonefish, Pacific Ocean

Some species of damselfish create true nuclear families within the same anemone. A couple's eggs are deposited and fertilized near the basal peduncle of the coelenterate, whose stinging tentacles guarantee an effective defense against most predators.

the substrate—which the nearly blind shrimp keeps clean and orderly while the fish acts as a guardian. The two species communicate according to a precise language: oscillating antennas for the shrimp and tail-fin vibrations for the goby. Still other shrimp—in the *Periclemenes*, *Lysmata* and *Stenopus* genera, not to mention fish (this time the labrids)— take the lead role in a complex symbiotic, mutualistic relationship that bonds the so-called "cleaners" to their "clients." Both partners

Dangerous Liaisons *In exchange for the protection they receive, damselfish strenuously defend their hosts from potential predators—as divers who get too close to anemones know all too well. They can testify to the minuscule fishes' courage in the face of much bigger intruders. The* Amphiprion *protect themselves from the effect of the anemones' stinging tentacles by augmenting the layer of mucus that envelops their skin; if it is somehow stripped away, however, they are quickly paralyzed and devoured.*

adhere to a complex ritual that serves a precise function. The cleaners, with their unmistakable banded coloration, position themselves in plain view in easily found locations in the open; the clients come to these "cleaning stations" and display a total lack of aggression while the cleaners remove parasites and leftover food from their skin, gills and mouth. The best known cleaner is the little *Labroides dimidiatus*, but young angelfish often perform the same function for large species. Examples of more or less symbiotic relationships among reef species are truly numerous. Less certain but apparently more commensal relationships are conducted between pelagic species like the *Echeneis naucrates* remora and the *Naucrates ductor* pilotfish and the big animals they routinely attend and whose advantage in this kind of relationship is far from obvious.

CONTRACTUAL ASSISTANCE

The alliances of more or less mutual collaboration drawn up by various species of fish or between a fish and an invertebrate are one of the most interesting and surprising aspects of the coral universe. If both of the "contracting parties" secure a benefit from the relationship, we speak of symbiosis (as in the case of damselfish and their anemones). If, instead, one of the two partners takes exclusive advantage of the situation, we speak of commensalism (pilotfish and remoras are a good example).

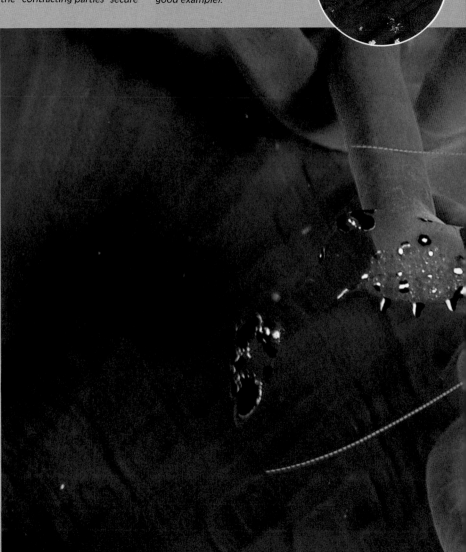

THE IMPORTANCE OF BEING CLEAN

Various fish and invertebrates actively perform the role of "cleaners" by removing tiny parasites, fragments of dead skin, damaged tissue, and bits of food from the skin, gills, and even the mouths of their "clients." A field experiment artificially removed cleaners from a tract of coral reef and showed that its inhabitants quickly registered a significant increase in infections and parasitism. The species dedicated to this activity—usually small labrids and shrimp, but certain young angelfish and butterflyfish as well—essentially enjoy total immunity. They can visit the mouths of predators such as groupers and morays whenever they like with no risk of being swallowed.

BURNING SKIN

There are those that exploit the advantages of a stinging host. Damselfish in the Amphiprion genus and various cleaner shrimps pass their entire existence under the tentacled protection of the great anemones while many young fish (carangids, for example) pass the first months of their lives swimming among the poisonous tentacles of various jellyfish.

A LITTLE MINDFULNESS

Too often, underwater photographers fail to realize the grave harm they cause the tiny creatures framed in their viewfinders. Anyone intending to photograph the minuscule crustaceans generally hosted by cushion star of the Culcita genus or many crinoids must avoid disturbing the subjects any more than necessary. In a moment of panic, they will often abandon the organism they live with and whose coloration they have assumed and immediately fall victim to some nearby predator. Some species—such as the almost blind shrimps that share a burrow in the seabed with a small, brightly colored goby—are completely incapable of survival if forcibly separated from their customary partner.

Spinecheek anemonefish
Premnas biaculeatus

Range Central Indo-Pacific
Habitat Coral seabeds,
3–15 m (10–50 ft)
Size Up to 14 cm (5.5 in)
Description Recognizable
by its big preopercular fin
and normally deep red or
dark orange coloration, the
female is much bigger than
the male. It lives in association with the anemones
Entacmaea quadricolor,
Heteractis crispa and *Sti-
chodactylus* spp.

240

Red saddleback anemonefish
Amphiprion ephippium

Range Andaman Sea, South
China Sea
Habitat Coral seabeds,
1–15 m (3–50 ft)
Size Up to 12 cm (4.75 in)
Description Usually found
in pairs, almost exclusively
in association with *Entacmaea quadricolor* and *Heteractis crispa* anemones.
Adults lack the white
bands found in immature
individuals.

Orange anemonefish
Amphiprion sandaracinos

Range Eastern Pacific Ocean
Habitat Coral seabeds, 6–20 m (20–65 ft)
Size Up to 12 cm (4.75 in)
Description Generally in pairs, often with numerous young in the same anemone. Found in a commensal relationship with *Heteractis crispa* and *Stichodactyla mertensii* anemones. Very similar to *A. akallopisos*, but more orange and less red.

Tomato anemonefish
Amphiprion frenatus

Range Central Indo-Pacific
Habitat Coral seabeds, 2–18 m (7–60 ft)
Size Up to 14 cm (5.5 in)
Description Adults can be identified by the single white band that crosses their cheeks vertically. Exclusively associated with the *Entacmaea quadricolor* anemone as are several other clownfish species.

Saddleback anemonefish
Amphiprion polymnus

Range Western Pacific Ocean
Habitat Sandy or silted seabeds, 3–35 m (10–115 ft)
Size Up to 13 cm (5 in)
Description An atypical species, which unlike others seems to prefer muddy or sandy seabeds, it is exclusively associated with the *Heteractis crispa* and *Stichodactyla haddoni* anemones. Its coloration is quite variable, but the one illustrated is the most common.

Clark's anemonefish
Amphiprion clarkii

Range Tropical Indo-Pacific
Habitat Coral seabeds, 1–20 m (3–65 ft)
Description Recognized by its black body crossed with three white stripes and accented to various degrees by yellow on its head, belly and fins. It is adapted to cohabitation with several anemones; its presence has been confirmed in more than ten different species.

Two-banded anemonefish
Amphiprion bicinctus

Range Red Sea, western Indian Ocean
Habitat Coral seabeds, 1–30 m (3–100 ft)
Size Up to 12 cm (4.75 in)
Description The only clownfish found in the Red Sea, usually associated with the *Entacmaea quadricolor*, *Heteractis aurora*, *H. crispa* and *Stichodactyla gigantea* anemones. Often in large aggregations with dozens of individuals, distributed on true "living carpets" composed of many large contiguous anemones.

Pink anemonefish
Amphiprion perideraion

302

Range Central Indo-Pacific
Habitat Coral seabeds, 3–15 m (10–50 ft)
Size Up to 10 cm (4 in)
Description This species adapts to life in association with various anemones, and is easily recognized by the longitudinal streak on its back and vertical band on its cheeks, both white on a delicate hot pink background.

Maldives anemonefish
Amphiprion nigripes

Range Indian Ocean
Habitat Coral seabeds, 2–25 m (7–80 ft)
Size Up to 11 cm (4.25 in)
Description The most common species from the Laccadive Islands archipelago to Sri Lanka and the Maldive Islands. Exclusively associated with the *Heteractis magnifica* anemone, often in large groups; recognizable by its black belly fins.

False clown anemonefish
Amphiprion ocellaris

Range Western Pacific Ocean
Habitat Coral seabeds, 1–15 m (3–50 ft)
Size Up to 8 cm (3 in)
Description Sometimes in small groups, in relationships with *Heteractis magnifica*, *Stichodactyla gigantea* and *S. mertensii* anemones. Replaced farther east by the *A. percula* species whose coloration is very similar.

Clown anemonefish
Amphiprion percula

 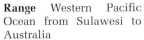 

Range Western Pacific Ocean from Sulawesi to Australia
Habitat Coral seabeds, 1–10 m (3–33 ft)
Size Up to 8 cm (3 in)
Description Often in small groups, in association with the same anemones that host the preceding species. Ground coloration is variable, sometimes violet or even black. Like all clownfish, it is highly prized by aquarists all over the world, although the task of maintaining this species correctly in captivity is rather complex.

245

Bluestreak cleaner wrasse
Labroides dimidiatus

Range Red Sea, tropical Indo-Pacific
Habitat Coral seabeds, 2–30 m (7–100 ft)
Size Up to 10 cm (4 in)
Description Extremely active as are most labrids, this species positions itself inside territory recognized by other fish as a kind of "free zone" where it cleans its visitors of external parasites and bits of dead skin. It is frequently observed probing the mouths of predators such as morays or groupers with impunity to feed on food scraps. The small blenny, *Aspidontus taeniatus*, imitates the cleaner's coloration and behavior perfectly in order to approach its victims and detach small bits of flesh or fragments of fin.

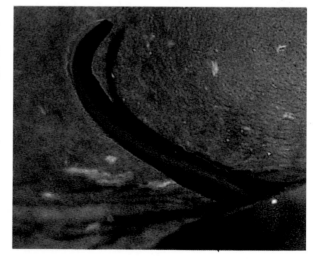

Sharksucker
Echeneis naucrates

Range Circumtropical, except the eastern Pacific
Habitat Open waters, 0.5–100 m (1.5–330 ft) and beyond
Size Up to 1 m (3 ft)
Description Common in warm waters, often in shallow water near coral reefs. The remora's modified dorsal fin (and its seven similar cousins) has become a laminate organ like a suction cup that it uses to adhere at will to the body of other species (usually sharks, but also turtles, rays, big labrids, boats and even divers) achieving effortless transportation. It usually feeds on its host's leftovers.

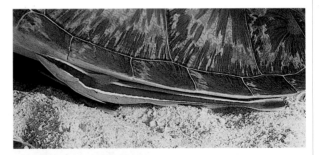

Spotted porcelain crab
Neopetrolisthes maculatus

Range Tropical Indo-Pacific
Habitat Coral seabeds in association with large anemones
Size Up to 7 cm (2.75 in)
Description Recognizable by its elegant, finely speckled coloration and its flattened claws, it is one of the species superficially similar to a crab but in reality closely related to the crinoid squat lobster that can normally be observed in pairs associated with the large sea anemones. Single individuals can apparently enter the oral cavity of the anemone that hosts them and exit at will without being devoured.

Symbiotic shrimp
Vir philippinensis

310

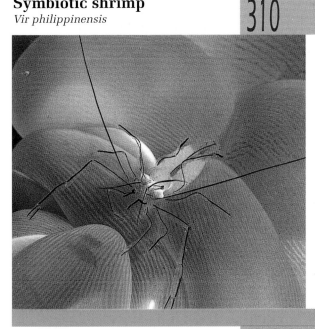

Range Tropical Indo-Pacific
Habitat Coral seabeds
Size Up to 2 cm (0.75 in)
Description Sometimes erroneously identified in the past with an indeterminate species of the *Periclemenes* genus, this elegant shrimp is immediately identifiable by its microhabitat and by its semitransparent body accented with violet along its legs, antennae and back. In fact, it lives exclusively in association with colonies of bubble coral, *Plerogyra sinuosa.*

Symbiotic shrimp
Periclemenes holthuisi

311

Range Red Sea, tropical Indo-Pacific
Habitat Coral seabeds in association with various hosts
Size Up to 2 cm (0.75 in)
Description This species of extraordinary beauty and elegance is found in association with a variety of hosts. It has been observed on several species of anemone, on the *Plerogyra* barrel coral, on colonies of *Fungia* mushroom coral and also on the belly portion of *Cassiopea* jellyfish. This shrimp occasionally assumes the cleaner role.

Pederson's cleaner shrimp
Periclemenes pedersoni

312

Range Tropical Atlantic Ocean, Caribbean Sea
Habitat Coral seabeds in association with anemones
Size Up to 2 cm (0.75 in)
Description A cleaner shrimp observed in association with the *Bartholomea annulata*, *Lebrunia danae*, *Condylactis gigantea* and *Heteractis lucida* anemones. Advertises its cleaner functions by standing in plain sight and making its long white antennae oscillate rhythmically.

Ambon cleaner shrimp
Thor amboinensis

313

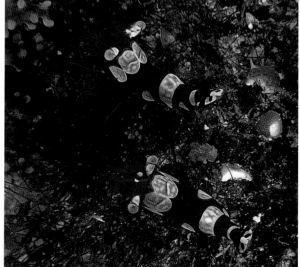

Range Tropical Indo-Pacific, Caribbean Sea
Habitat Coral seabeds in association with anemones
Size Up to 1 cm (0.5 in)
Description Recognized by its yellowish base color and the opalescent saddles that adorn its back; in association with various species of corals and anemones, especially *Actinodendrum glomeratum*, among whose tentacles it can often be observed in small groups composed of two to eight individuals. Females grow to double the size of males.

Imperial shrimp
Periclemenes imperator

Range Red Sea, tropical Indo-Pacific

Habitat Coral seabeds in association with various hosts

Size Up to 1 cm (0.5 in)

Description A species with a variable coloration recognizable by its flattened frontal laminae, observable with relative frequency in association with various hosts. It is commensal with the so-called Spanish dancer (a large nudibranch) *Hexabranchus sanguineus*, on whose feces it feeds, and with large sea cucumbers classified in the *Stichopus*, *Bohadschia* and *Synapta* genera. Also observed in association with starfish in the *Gomophia* genus.

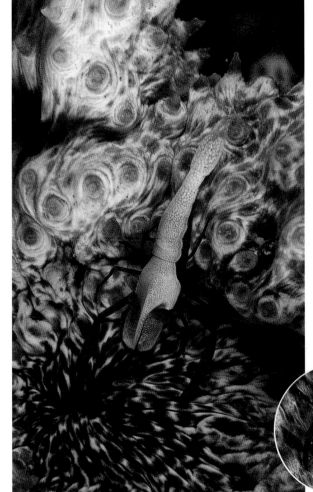

Symbiotic shrimp
Periclemenes soror

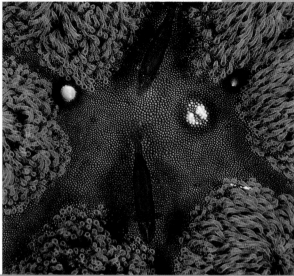

Range Red Sea, tropical Indo-Pacific
Habitat Coral seabeds in association with starfish
Size Up to 5 mm (0.25 in)
Description A minuscule commensal shrimp with a highly variable coloration, generally observable on the ventral and dorsal fascia of big starfish in the *Culcita*, *Acanthaster*, *Choriaster* and *Linckia* genera. The individual's coloration is closely related to that of the host organism.

Anemone shrimp
Periclemenes brevicarpalis

Range Red Sea, tropical Indo-Pacific
Habitat Coral seabeds in association with large anemones
Size Up to 4 cm (1.5 in)
Description One of the larger species of symbiotic shrimps characterized by the big white blotch on its cephalothorax. Usually associated with the large, flat anemone, *Cryptodendrum adhaesivum*, in which it cohabits with the Clark clownfish, *Amphiprion clarkii*.

Symbiotic shrimp
Periclemenes kororensis

Range Central Indo-Pacific
Habitat Coral seabeds in association with anemones
Size Up to 4 cm (1.5 in)
Description This species is rather difficult to spot and has a transparent body and claws and a conspicuous white head. Because it keeps its abdomen hidden, it looks more like a crab than a shrimp. Observed in association with various species of anemone.

Crinoid squat lobster
Allogalathea elegans

Range Tropical Indo-Pacific
Habitat Coral seabeds in association with crinoids
Size Up to 2 cm (0.75 in)
Description A small crustacean that lives exclusively in association with various species of crinoids (see page 166), its coloration varies according to the host organism. The females of the species are normally larger. Perfectly adapted to its host and therefore completely incapable of survival if separated from it.

RELATIONSHIPS

Symbiotic shrimp
Periclemenes ceratophthalmus

Range Tropical Indo-Pacific
Habitat Coral seabeds in association with crinoids
Size Up to 1 cm (0.5 in)
Description A rather common but extremely mimetic shrimp, its coloration varies radically in relation to the crinoid that hosts it. Exclusively found among the threads of crinoids in the *Himerometra, Dichrometra* and *Lamprometra* genera (see page 166). Its habits and needs are substantially the same as those of the *Allogalathea elegans*.

254

Spider crab
Naxioides taurus

Range Andaman Sea, eastern Pacific Ocean
Habitat Coral seabeds in association with soft corals
Size Up to 2 cm (0.75 in)
Description This species has an inconspicuous coloration, is often covered with hydroids, and is recognized by its bifurcated beak; frequently found in association with soft corals in the *Dendronephtya* genus.

Symbiotic shrimp
Pontonides unciger

Range Red Sea, tropical Indo-Pacific

Habitat Coral seabeds in a relationship with black coral

Size Up to 15 mm (0.5 in)

Description This tiny shrimp is found exclusively in association with colonies of black coral in the genus *Cirripathes*, where it has evolved a superbly mimetic banded coloration for camouflage.

Sea whip gobies
Bryaninops sp.

Range Red Sea, tropical Indo-Pacific

Habitat Coral seabeds in association with whip corals

Size Up to 4 cm (1.5 in)

Description The various species of *Bryaninops* gobies, all rather similar, live nearly exclusively in association with whip corals and sea fans of the *Juncella* and *Elisella* genera, sometimes in colonies of black coral, *Antipathes dichotoma*, and much more rarely on tabular formations of *Acropora*. They feed on zooplankton.

RELATIONSHIPS

BENTHIC SPECIES

LIFE ON THE SEABED

The environment on the sea floor to which benthic species are closely bound is richly populated with animals of great interest. Not only fish—such as goatfish, moray eels, rays, sole, blennies, and gobies—but also and mostly crustaceans, mollusks and invertebrates in general. Many of these species are wary, however, and have twilight or nocturnal habits that make observation difficult. Others are known as sessile—fixed to the substrate, such as bivalves—and are often ignored in favor of creatures that are more spectacular. In reality, however, the benthic microenvironment may produce more themes of interest. It is on sandy, silted or rubbly seabeds, in fact, where fascinating symbiotic interactions take place between little nesting gobies and their roommates, the alpheid shrimps (see page 144). And it is often here that species with the most remarkable mimetic abilities lie motionless in ambush (see page 218). It is also here that the amazing colors of nudibranchs can be viewed (see pages 160 to 165). The echinoderms (with sea urchins and starfish among the standouts) display some of the most surprising shapes and colors on the reef while few ichthyic species can rival the flourish of the big *Tridacna*'s mantle or the chromatics of noctur-

Often ignored by divers in favor of larger species, the creatures whose life cycles are rigorously bound to the bottom—such as many crustaceans and mollusks—often exhibit bizarre shapes and colors that are fascinating and of great beauty. Below, a Saron *genus crab.*

Beautiful and Deadly

The reef animals that pose the most potential danger are probably not the large, much-feared predators such as sharks. More perilous and far more terrifying creatures hide in the seabed and come forth only under cover of darkness. Other than mantis prawns (at right), whose fearsome looks and predatory habits are mitigated only by their reduced size, tropical seabeds are host to truly dangerous creatures like the conchs in the Conus *genus. These gastropods have a proboscis they use to "shoot" poisonous darts into their prey. Their poison can also be lethal to humans.*

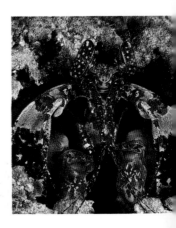

nal prawns in the genus *Saron* or the common reef mantis, *Odontodactylus scyllaris*. The benthic environment—whose populations are closely tied to the concept of depth—is very complex. It would require a more detailed examination to fully understand the variety of species living in the depths. Therefore, this chapter merely groups together some of the most easily observed species in an exploration of the reef.

There is no shortage of interesting fish species on the bottom, but this area covered with coralline detritus is really the uncontested kingdom of mollusks and crustaceans.

PHOTOGENIC

Among all the bivalves found in tropical waters, members of the Tridacna *genus may be the* most photogenic. They include many species and owe their appeal to the marvelous and highly variable coloration of their mantle (the fleshy part exposed when their valves are open). Bivalves lack the gastropods' characteristic radula (a tongue with teeth that snails use to procure food) and have evolved a gill system that filters plankton from the water and carries out respiratory functions. Other bivalves capture

their prey by rapidly contracting a modified gill.

TOOTHED TONGUE
Sea snails (like land snails) belong to the gastropod ("feet on the belly") class. The biggest is the Syrinx aruanus, an Indonesian snail that reaches lengths of 90 centimeters (35 inches), but most are much smaller. These are extremely sophisticated predators whose principal trait is the radula, a semi-rigid tongue covered with teeth (up to 750,000) used to capture and ingest its prey.

FILTER FEEDING
Bivalves are filtering animals that aspirate water through one siphon and expel it through another (see inset photos) having first extracted suspended nutrients and the oxygen needed to breathe. Bivalves in the Tridacna genus also avail themselves of symbiotic single-celled algae (zooxanthellae) in their tissues to increase the availability of energy, in the same way that corals do. The lively hues of the giant clams are caused by these zooxanthellae. Since many bivalves are securely attached to the substrate, their reproduction is accomplished with the simultaneous release of millions of eggs and spermatic cells.

SPOOKY
Some tropical worms look as if they were straight out of a horror movie. Members of the Eunice genus grow as much as 9 meters (30 feet) long but only 25 mm (1 inch) in diameter. They are furnished with five pairs of enormous traplike jaws that they use to capture the fish they eat. They live on sandy bottoms at a depth of one or two meters.

Spotted prawn
Saron sp.

323

Range Red Sea, tropical Indo-Pacific
Habitat Rubbly bottoms and slopes, 1–30 m (3–100 ft)
Size Up to 15 cm (6 in)
Description The five separate known species display extraordinary beauty and unusual mimetic skills that, together with their nocturnal habits, make them hard to see. Beyond their characteristic spotted design, members of the *Saron* genus are also often characterized by one or a series of bristles on their beaks and along their backs.

Banded coral shrimp
Stenopus hispidus

324

Range Red Sea, central Indo-Pacific
Habitat Coral seabeds, 5–35 m (16–115 ft)
Size Up to 5 cm (2 in)
Description An unmistakable cleaner shrimp with its characteristic red- and white-banded coloration; it announces its availability by positioning itself in front of fissures and hollows and oscillating its long white antennas. During the day it prefers protected sites, so it is easier to observe at night in the open. It generally lives in stable pairs.

Striped cleaner prawn
Lysmata amboinensis

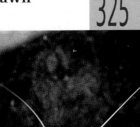

Range Red Sea, tropical Indo-Pacific
Habitat Coral seabeds, 5–35 m (16–115 ft)
Size Up to 5 cm (2 in)
Description A cleaner shrimp whose behavior is very similar to the *Stenopus hispidus*, except that it seems to have somewhat more gregarious habits. It is also found in the tropical Atlantic and in the Caribbean, where it is actually classified as *L. grabhami*.

Hingebeak prawn
Rhynchocinetes sp.

Range Central Indo-Pacific
Habitat Coral drop-offs, 5–30 m (16–100 ft)
Size Up to 4 cm (1.5 in)
Description This species' classification is still being defined; it is recognizable by its long beak and big eyes. Relatively common in the places where it has been observed but not often noted because of its largely nocturnal habits.

Hingebeak prawn
Rhynchocinetes durbanensis

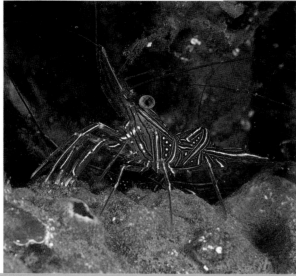

Range Central Indo-Pacific
Habitat Crevices and hollows, 5–35 m (16–115 ft)
Size Up to 4 cm (1.5 in)
Description Very similar to its cousins *R. uritai* and *R. brucei*, this vividly colored prawn has skittering movements and is characteristic of fissures and crevices, inside of which it is often observable in groups made up of dozens of individuals.

Royal crab
Mithrax spinosissimus

Range Caribbean Sea
Habitat Sandy and coralline seabeds, 1–30 m (3–100 ft)
Size Up to 30 cm (12 in)
Description This large crab with a shell bristling with nodules and spines is found in rocky areas and on reefs. Usually takes refuge in crevices and cracks during the day; in the open at night, often on sandy flats, in search of food. Territorial; adults often confront each other in ritualized duels. Known locally by a variety of different popular names.

Arrow crab
Stenorhynchus seticornis

Range Caribbean Sea
Habitat Coral seabeds, 1–30 m (3–100 ft)
Size Up to 5 cm (2 in)
Description This tiny, brightly colored crab is characterized by extraordinarily long and slender limbs and by its pointed cephalic beak. It can be approached without difficulty both day and night; frequently seen on sea fans and inside the calyx-type sponges characteristic of Caribbean seabeds.

Red coral crab
Carpilius convexus

Range Tropical Indo-Pacific
Habitat Coral seabeds
Size Up to 20 cm (8 in)
Description Also classified by some sources as *Altergatis subdentatus*, it is characterized by its red-orange shell decorated by a darker spot in the center. Nocturnal in habit, it is very similar in behavior and form to its cousin *C. maculatus*, whose carapace is decorated by seven roundish dark spots.

Common reef mantis
Odontodactylus scyllaris

Range Tropical Indo-Pacific
Habitat Areas of detritus and sandy bottoms, 1–70 m (3–230 ft)
Size Up to 25 cm (10 in)
Description This fast, active nocturnal predator hunts outside its den feeding on mollusks, fish and other crustaceans. It can inflict painful wounds with its raptorial front limbs. It has an intense warning coloration that probably makes it one of the most brightly colored species of crustacean in the world. Avoid disturbing it or brushing up against it. Its front limbs strike their prey with the force of a .22 caliber bullet.

They did not earn their worldwide "thumbcracker" nickname by

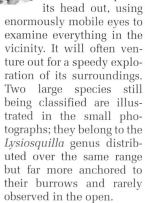

accident! By day, the mantis stands in a burrow dug into the substrate; it pokes its head out, using enormously mobile eyes to examine everything in the vicinity. It will often venture out for a speedy exploration of its surroundings. Two large species still being classified are illustrated in the small photographs; they belong to the *Lysiosquilla* genus distributed over the same range but far more anchored to their burrows and rarely observed in the open.

Lobster
Palinurus sp.

Range Circumtropical
Habitat Coral and rocky seabeds, 1–50 m (3–165 ft)
Size Up to 40 cm (16 in)

Description The *Palinurus* genus (often erroneously transcribed as *Panulirus*) is represented by numerous species in all the world's tropical and subtropical seas. It is a predatory, nocturnal animal with a vividly decorated coat. They are often numerous locally; they linger in crevices (with their long antennas sticking out) during the day and hunt small benthic organisms at night, but they also feed on organic detritus when they happen across it. Lobsters have recently suffered a dramatic demographic decline; entire populations have been annihilated by intensive fishing, especially where tourism abounds.

Tiger cowrie
Cypraea tigris

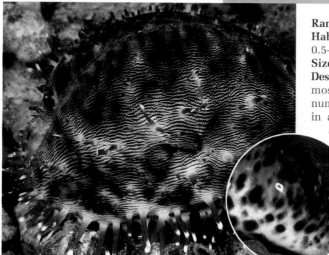

Range Tropical Indo-Pacific
Habitat Coral seabeds, 0.5–10 m (1.5–33 ft)
Size Up to 7 cm (2.75 in)
Description Perhaps the most common of the numerous *Cypraea*, found in all tropical seas. Hides among corals during the day, and hunts at night on the bottom in search of prey (sponges and benthic organisms). Normally, the conch and its porcelain surface are covered by its extended mantle.

268

Flamingo tongue cowrie
Cyphoma gibbosum

Range Caribbean Sea
Habitat Coral seabeds, 2–15 m (7–50 ft)
Size Up to 2 cm (0.75 in)
Description A small, elegant gastropod whose cream-colored shell is normally covered by a characteristically yellow-orange spotted mantle. Very common locally; easily observed on fronds of the violet sea fan, *G. ventalina*, whose polyps it feeds on. The *C. signatum* species, with finely striated spots, is more rare.

Triton's trumpet
Charonia tritonis

335

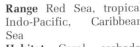

Range Red Sea, tropical Indo-Pacific, Caribbean Sea
Habitat Coral seabeds, 3–40 m (10–130 ft)
Size Up to 50 cm (20 in)
Description One of the best known and most resplendent of tropical marine gastropods, this large predatory mollusk usually feeds on echinoderms. The dangerous crown-of-thorns starfish, *Acanthaster planci*, which feeds on coral polyps, figures among its prey. It is a protected species and many countries prohibit its harvest.

269

Christmas tree worm
Spirobranchus giganteus

336

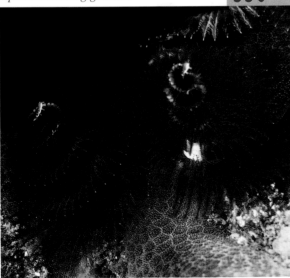

Range Circumtropical
Habitat Coral seabeds, 1–40 m (3–130 ft)
Size Up to 3 cm (1 in)
Description The characteristic spiraling and multicolored "little umbrellas" protruding from madreporic colonies (usually *Porites*) are actually the ruffled gills of a small worm hidden in a tube hollowed out of the coral. Very sensitive to variations in light and water pressure, it retreats into its tube with lightning speed if threatened. It feeds on suspended microplankton.

Giant clams
Tridacna sp.

Range Red Sea, tropical Indo-Pacific

Habitat Coral seabeds, 0.5–15 m (1.5–50 ft)

Size Up to 1.3 m (4.25 ft)

Description Diverse *Tridacna* species share the characteristic undulating rims and stratified outer surface of their valves. The bright fluorescent color of their mantle is created by the presence of unicellular symbiotic algae, or zooxanthellae. The species illustrated is *T. gigas*, the biggest and heaviest, which can grow to 250 kilograms (550 pounds) in weight. It has become rare following the intense commercial fishery to which it has been subjected in recent years throughout the Pacific Ocean.

Golden thorny oyster
Spondylus aurantius

Range Red Sea, tropical Indo-Pacific
Habitat Seaward reef slopes, 10–40 m (33–130 ft)
Size About 30 cm (12 in)
Description This big bivalve is very similar to an oyster but more vividly colored. Found most often tenaciously clinging to the reef wall and covered externally by a multitude of sessile organisms. Its orange-colored mantle is decorated with blue ocelli.

Cock's comb oyster
Lopha cristagalli

339

Range Red Sea, tropical Indo-Pacific
Habitat Slopes on seaward reefs, 15–50 m (50–165 ft)
Size Up to 20 cm (8 in)
Description This species attaches itself to the branches of sea fans and anthozoans in deep waters where currents are strong. Its valves are covered with sponges and encrusting red sea squirts. Recognizable by the characteristic zigzagging rim of its valves.

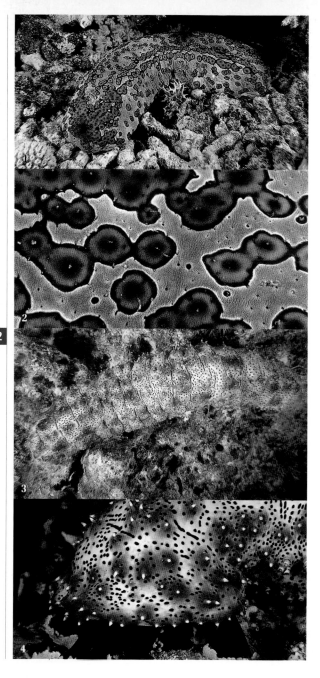

HOLOTHURIANS

These echinoderms, commonly called sea cucumbers, have developed an elongated and subcylindrical shape while maintaining their typical pentagonal symmetry in section. They lie on the sandy bottom with one side of their body facing down, and, unlike other echinoderms, have a "head" and a "tail." They are predominantly diurnal; they feed on benthic detritus that they gather up along with large quantities of sand, using adhesive tentacles that rim the oral aperture. Beyond producing toxic substances, they can expel long whitish and sticky filaments, which ultimately thwart the movements of a predator. This form of self-defense does not save them from humans, however, who fish them in large numbers and, after drying them, use them as a precious ingredient known as *trepang* or *bêche-de-mer* in Chinese cuisine. This practice has wiped out entire populations, putting the species' survival at risk in many areas. Various commensal species are commonly seen among the tubercles and nodules that adorn the bodies of holothurians. The most common and interesting is the symbiotic shrimp, *Periclemenes imperator* (see page 251), which—though it sports a completely different coloration—is also often found near the gill tufts of the large nudibranch, *Hexabranchus sanguineus*.

1. *Bohadschia argus*
Range Tropical Indo-Pacific
Size Up to 35 cm (14 in)

2. *Bohadschia argus*
Range Tropical Indo-Pacific
Size Up to 35 cm (14 in)

3. *Bohadschia graeffei*
Range Red Sea, tropical Indo-Pacific
Size Up to 35 cm (14 in)

4. *Bohadschia graeffei*
Range Red Sea, tropical Indo-Pacific
Size Up to 35 cm (14 in)

5. *Thelenota ananas*
Range Tropical Indo-Pacific
Size Up to 50 cm (20 in)

6. *Thelenota ananas*
Range Tropical Indo-Pacific
Size Up to 50 cm (20 in)

7. *Stichopus chloronotus*
Range Tropical Indo-Pacific
Size Up to 40 cm (16 in)

8. *Periclemenes imperator*
Range Tropical Indo-Pacific
Size Up to 1 cm (0.5 in)

Holothurians

THE EXPOSED PART OF THE REEF

The stretches of dry land opposite a coral reef are intimately bound to it whether they are beaches, estuaries, rocky outcroppings or mangrove forests. An exploration of all these environments, where the boundaries of land and sea are often blurred, would not fail to hold surprises. Especially in southeast Asia, there are many places where it is possible to come across interesting reptiles. First of all are the sea snakes, *Laticauda colubrina*; they are venomous but usually docile and display a banded coloration alternately gray-blue and black and a tail that is paddle-shaped at the tip, denoting the species' almost exclusively aquatic habits. You can sometimes come across turtles that are busy digging their nests or depositing eggs. Disturbing them during this activity, however, risks their immediate return to the water and jeopardizes the incubation. One most often finds the green turtle, *Chelonia mydas,* but in some locations (especially in Malaysia and Costa Rica) it is also possible to observe the gigantic lute or leatherback turtle, *Dermochelys coriacea.* A far more dangerous reptile frequents the estuaries, mangrove forests, and brackish waters, sometimes traveling a considerable distance from the coast. A predator as long as 7 meters (23 feet), the

1. Leatherback Turtle
Dermochelys coriacea
Range Cosmopolitan
Size Up to 2 m (6.5 ft)

2. Coconut Crab
Birgus latro
Range Tropical Indo-Pacific
Size Up to 40 cm (16 in)

3. Yellow-Lipped Sea Snake
Laticauda colubrina
Range Red Sea, tropical Indo-Pacific
Size Up to 1.8 m (6 ft)

4. Marine Crocodile
Crocodylus porosus
Range Tropical Indo-Pacific
Size Up to 7 m (23 ft)

5. Green Turtle
Chelonia mydas
Range Tropical Indo-Pacific
Size Up to 1.4 m (4.5 ft)

6. Brown Noddy
Anous stolidus
Range Tropical Indo-Pacific
Size Wingspan up to 40 cm (16 in)

7. Magnificent Frigatebird
Fregata magnificens
Range Cosmopolitan
Size Wingspan up to 2 m (6.5 ft)

8. Brown Booby
Sula leucogaster
Range Cosmopolitan
Size Wingspan up to 1.5 m (5 ft)

The Exposed Part of the Reef

marine or estuary crocodile, *Crocodylus porosus*, does not hesitate to attack humans. The mangrove forests host less terrifying creatures, too, including the mudskippers of the *Periophtalmus* genus, a fish up to 20 cm (8 in) long that can survive at length out of water. They are easily observed as they engage in ritual duels to defend territory among the mangrove's characteristic aerial roots— called pneumatophores— that grow densely out of the ground. Mangroves in the *Rizophora* genus prefer muddy bottoms and are therefore sparse on coral beaches. Easier to observe are the coconut palm, *Cocos nucifera*, and the screw pine, *Pandanus*, two species that could also colonize the most remote oceanic locations. In southeast Asia, a large crustacean can sometimes be found among the intricate roots at their base. The coconut crab, *Birgus latro*, is nocturnal and can grow to more than 40 cm (16 in) in diameter. Depending upon the geographic zone, various species of pelicans, seagulls, herons (and the gray heron, *Ardea cinerea*, stands out), flamingoes and boobies can be observed. Other birds such as the frigatebird, *Fregata magnificens*, are dispersed circumtropically so they can be observed just about everywhere.

9. Brown Pelican
Pelecanus occidentalis
Range Atlantic Ocean
Size Wingspan up to 2 m
(6.5 ft)

10. Sooty Tern
Sterna fuscata
Range Tropical Indo-Pacific
Size Wingspan up to
40 cm (16 in)

11. Mangrove
Rizophora sp.
Range Cosmopolitan
Size Up to 8 m (26 ft)

12. Intertidal zone
exposed at low tide

13. Coconut Palm
Cocos nucifera
Range Cosmopolitan
Size Up to 10 m (33 ft)

14. Screw Pine
Pandanus sp.
Range Tropical Indo-Pacific
Size Up to 4 m (13 ft)

15. Flamingo
Phoenicopterus ruber
Range Atlantic Ocean
Size Wingspan up to 2 m
(6.5 ft)

16. Tracks left by a turtle
after depositing its eggs on
the beach.

APPENDICES

INDEX

285

BIBLIOGRAPHY

Marine Animals of Baja California
Daniel W. Gotshall, Sea
Challengers, 1982

*Ambiente e Pesci dei Mari
Tropicali* (Habitats and Fish of
Tropical Seas)
Enrico Tortonese, Calderini, 1983

Marine Life of the Caribbean
James Cribb, Jacques-Yves
Cousteau & Thomas H.
Suchanek, SkyLine Press, 1984

Red Sea Reef Fishes
John E. Randall, Immel
Publishing, 1986

Sharks of Arabia
John E. Randall, Immel
Publishing, 1986

Reef Fishes of the Indian Ocean
Gerald R. Allen & Roger C.
Steene, T.F.H. Publications, 1987

*Unterwasserfuhrer Rotes
Meer—Fische* (Underwater
Guide to the Fish of the Red Sea)
Helmut Debelius, Verlag
Stephanie Naglschmid, 1987

*Unterwasserfuhrer Rotes
Meer—Niedere Tiere*
(Underwater Guide to Benthic
Species of the Red Sea)
Peter Schmid & Dieter Paschke,
Verlag Stephanie Naglschmid,
1987

Micronesian Reef Fishes
Robert F. Myers, Coral Graphics,
1991

*Unterwasserfuhrer Malediven—
Fische* (Underwater Guide to
Fish of the Maldives)
Peter Nahke & Peter Wirtz,
Verlag Stephanie Naglschmid,
1991

*Diver's Guide to the Sharks
of the Maldives*
R.C. Anderson, Novelty
Publications, 1992

*An Underwater Guide to
the South China Sea*
Chou Loke Ming & Porfirio M.
Alino, Times Editions, 1992

Fishes of the Maldives
John E. Randall, Immel
Publishing, 1992

Underwater Indonesia
Kal Muller, PeriplusEditions,
1992

*Southeast Asia Tropical Fish
Guide*
Rudie H. Kuiter & Helmut
Debelius, IKAN Unterwasserar-
chiv, 1994

*La barriera corallina—Guida al
mondo dei coralli* (The Coral
Reef—Guide to the Coral
World)
Angelo Mojetta, Edizioni White
Star, 1995

Sharks
Doug Perrine, WorldLife Library,
1995

*Coral Reef Animals of the
Indo-Pacific*
Terrence M. Gosliner, David W.
Behrens & Gary C. Williams, Sea
Challengers, 1996

Pesci e coralli del mar rosso
(Red Sea Fish and Corals)
Angelo Mojetta & Andrea
Ghisotti, Mondadori, 1996

*Nudibranchs and Sea Snails
Indo-Pacific Field Guide*
Helmut Debelius, IKAN
Unterwasserarchiv, 1996

Il mio mar rosso (My Red Sea)
Folco Quilici, Mondadori, 1998

Oceani (Oceans)
Edited by Angelo Mojetta,
Mondadori, 1998

Squali (Sharks)
Piero and Alberto Angela &
Alberto Luca Recchi,
Mondadori, 1998

Living Reefs of the Maldives
R.C. Anderson, Novelty
Publications

Reef Creature Identification
Paul Humann, New World
Publications

Reef Fish Identification
Paul Humann, New World
Publications

NAVIGATING THE INTERNET IN SEARCH OF THE REEF

These days, to our good fortune, a nearly infinite quantity of information is available to everyone on the Net. Anyone interested in acquiring more specific information about the topics presented in this book can surf the Web with success and satisfaction by visiting the sites listed below. Some refer to important academic and scientific institutions, others to associations actively involved on the front line of environmental advocacy and protection. All are extremely interesting and—even more important—rich in data and starting points for a more comprehensive study. Since these sites are managed by large organizations, it is less likely that the URLs will be changed without notice.

Aquatic Conservation Network
http://www.acn.ca/index.html

Australian Institute of Marine Science
http://ibm590.aims.gov.au/

International Marine Mammal Association
http://www.imma.org/

Ocean Planet
http://seawifs.gsfc.nasa.gov/ocean_planet.html

Ocean Voice International
http://www.ovi.ca

Reef Relief
http://www.reefrelief.org/

IREEF Resource Page
http://www.ualberta.ca/pblancho/index.html

Stazione Zoologica "Anton Dohrn"
http://www.szn.it

The Coral Health and Monitoring Program
http://coral.aoml.noaa.gov/

The Coral Reef Alliance
http://www.coralreefalliance.org

The Cousteau Society
http://www.cousteausociety.org

The Dolphin Society
http://www.dolphinsoc.org/

The Marine Mammal Center
http://www.tmmc.org/

The Smithsonian Institute
http://www.si.edu/

Woods Hole Oceanographic Institution
http://www.whoi.edu/

World Conservation Monitoring Centre
http://www.unep-wcmc.org